inviting God
to your wedding

Blessings!
Martha
Williamson

Inviting God

The executive producer
of the inspiring television series
"Touched By An Angel"
shares insights to help brides and grooms
prepare spiritually for their weddings.

to Your Wedding

and Keeping God in Your Marriage

MARTHA WILLIAMSON

with a chapter for men by

JON ANDERSEN

 Three Rivers Press NEW YORK

For permissions, see page 265

Library of Congress Cataloging-in-Publication Data

Williamson, Martha.
  Inviting God to your wedding / by Martha Williamson.
  1. Marriage—Religious aspects—Christianity.   I. Title.
BV835.W56 2000
265'.5—dc21
                                                    00-021535
                ISBN 978-0-307-58769-5

Printed in the United States of America

Design by Lynne Amft

10 9 8 7 6 5 4 3 2 1

First Paperback Edition

This book is lovingly and gratefully dedicated to

Pastor Jack and Anna Hayford.

When we wanted to invite God to our wedding,

they showed us how;

and

to my husband, Jon Andersen,

whose invitation to the Almighty changed our lives forever.

Acknowledgments

I AM ESPECIALLY GRATEFUL TO ALL MY WONDERFUL friends who contributed their time, their love, their wisdom, and their prayers to this little book:

Many thanks to my agent, Loretta Barrett, who first believed in this book, to Linda Loewenthal, who fought for this book, and to Shaye Areheart, who survived this book. To all my new friends at Harmony Books, especially Anne Berry and Kate Kennedy. To our own CBS family, and to my friend Leigh Brecheen.

My love to Carol Visser, Bob and Mary Salisbury, Karen and Jim Covell, Lisa and Russell Hilliard, Alan and Judy Johnson, Ruthie Webster, Dawn and Jim O'Keeffe, Barry and Judy Rogers, Karla Molk, Barbara and Eric Andersen, Don and Betty Fuchs, Marlene and Vince Shryack, Nina and Ron White, Kim and David Kuo, and other wonderful friends who took the time to share their wedding memories with us.

My deepest gratitude to Brandi Harkonen, Lisa Dolab, David Caruso, Luke Schelhaas, Jeanne Quan, and Angela Held for their generosity, incredible love and support, for the sleepless nights, the prayers, the suggestions, the good humor, and the loyalty.

To Jim Evans, Chris Easterly, Ross Jutsum, and Kathy Berg for giving extra time, great spirit, and commitment to this project.

My deep appreciation to the writers, producers, cast, and crew of *Touched By An Angel* for holding down the fort.

ACKNOWLEDGMENTS

My heartfelt thanks to Sonya Dunn Hodson and Suzonne Stirling Glassberg. I will always be grateful for the creativity and hard work you put into making our wedding day the happiest day of our lives.

To the talented photographers Beth Herzhaft, Judy Margolin, Neil Bloomquist, and David Witte.

To Sonya and Jim Hodson for introducing us to *Clowning in Rome.*

To Indy. You were missed. Welcome back.

To Randy and Elizabeth Travis for their amazing grace.

Eternal love and gratitude to my family, especially my sisters and my mother, whose love and support for my various ventures have never failed.

To our daughters, Isabel and Abigail, who turned a happy marriage into a happy family.

And finally to Marcie Gold, whose wisdom, unshakable faithfulness to God, and extraordinary commitment to friendship got this book to press . . . twice! May God bless you in His own time, Marcie Anne, with the man of your dreams.

Contents

III
the engagement
and planning for the big day
113

IV
the big day
177

The day we were married it rained. It rained so hard, there was a waterfall on the altar. It rained so hard that the bridge to our honeymoon cottage collapsed. It rained so hard that the police had trouble finding the armed fugitive who was hiding some-where in the vicinity of the reception tent. It rained so hard that there was nothing to do but pray. But by then, we were good at talking with God. We had invited God to our wedding a long time ago, and no matter what happened, we knew He would show up.

He did.

inviting God
to your wedding

introduction

God is the silent partner
in all great enterprises.
ABRAHAM LINCOLN

Therefore everyone who hears His words and puts them
into practice is like a wise man who built his house on the
rock. The rain came down, the streams rose, and the winds
blew and beat against that house; yet it did not fall, because
it had its foundation on the rock.
MATTHEW 7:24–25

THE WEDDING BOOK I COULDN'T FIND

In the months before our wedding, I searched the shelves of
my favorite bookstores for a wedding book that I never found: a
book that would celebrate my joy and acknowledge my fears.
A book that would be a silent friend who wouldn't overwhelm
me with week-by-week checklists and endless pictures of table
settings and chairs that looked like gold bamboo. I knew that
before I began organizing the most important event of my life,
I needed to organize my heart. Soon I discovered that my fiancé,
Jon, was looking for the very same book. We both needed

help deciding not how big the wedding should be, not how much it should cost or where it should take place, but how we could make it meaningful to us and to those we would gather around us.

How many times have I attended a wedding that was a performance piece, a theatrical event instead of a sacred occasion? I have sat through many years of quick ceremonies and blowout parties, Camelot theme weddings, and the beautiful but bewildering "virtual weddings" that were all style and no content. Often I recognize calligraphy on a large white envelope among the junk mail and sigh, "Oh no, . . . another wedding."

It seemed to me that many weddings had become a substitute for the prom or the Oscars or the Miss America pageant or whatever dream had never been fulfilled. The wedding day had been transformed into a chance to even the score with a captive audience summoned to attend for the purposes of being impressed by money or size or creativity rather than being included at the moment of a precious miracle.

And a miracle is exactly what a marriage can be. We are all married in the sight of God, but if you invite Him to the wedding and the preparations, being married in the *presence* of God is a wholly different experience. Because when God is there, suddenly all of your priorities are in order. You become less concerned about losing ten pounds before the last fitting. You're not worried if it rains. Your highest priority is to get ready spiritually.

ARE YOU READY?

Are you ready to forget the old boyfriends? To throw away the love letters and the mementos of past relationships that can damage your marriage? Are you ready to say no to the toxic guest who will certainly spend the reception wondering how long the two of you will last? Are you ready to laugh when the cake is chocolate instead of lemon? Are you ready to cry when you need to cry instead of protecting your make-up? Are you ready to allow your fiancé's dreams for his wedding to change the dreams you've always had for yours? Are you ready to be a hostess at your wedding rather than a princess?

Why would you put on a new dress and new shoes but get married with an old heart? Don't you want to feel as beautiful and new inside as you will look on the outside? Are you ready to invite the One Guest who can perform that miracle? I believe God wants to be there. His love and concern for His children will help you and your fiancé get ready for a lifetime together.

TYING THE KNOT A NEW WAY
A cord of three strands is not easily torn apart.
ECCLESIASTES 4:12

Remember when you first learned to braid your hair as a child? You only had two little hands, so you tried to twist just two unwieldy strands together. Remember how quickly it all fell apart? Then someone showed you how to weave three strands together and secure it. It was tight and beautiful. You couldn't tell where one strand stopped and the other began. And it took real effort to separate the three pieces again.

If you remember anything about this book, remember this: If you invite God to your wedding, He'll become the third strand, the one that strengthens the bond you and your husband will create on your wedding day. And when the occasional storms or everyday tempests of life threaten to unravel the precious knot He has tied, He will be the strand that holds the other two together.

PREPARE YOUR HEART

At the end of the day, after the phone calls to the florist, the faxes to the caterer, the explanations to the bridesmaids, the negotiations with the mothers, and the planning sessions with your fiancé, it is my guess that your brain has been in charge of the wedding all day. Give your heart some time now.

Don't cheat your heart out of the joy of preparing for the big day. It needs to get organized, too.

HOW TO USE THIS BOOK

It is our hope that this small volume will be an oasis in the busy months of preparation for your wedding. We would like to think it will offer you a chapter a night to read and consider and reread, right up until your very special day.

Try reading just a few pages of this book every night. Flip to the subject that's on your mind, and take a few minutes to look at it, asking God to be with you. Remember, the first thing He ever did was bring order out of chaos!

Whether or not you agree with everything we suggest, consider each chapter to be a challenge to look at the details of planning your wedding in a whole new way: Instead of planning for a wedding, start planning for a miracle.

I bought dozens of wedding books and never read a single one all the way through. I flipped through the books, looking for pictures that I liked. I flipped through the book of wedding readings. I flipped through the etiquette books. However, there was one book I would have gladly read from cover to cover, and that was a book that would help me include God in our wedding. I was looking for encouragement. I was looking for reassurance. And mostly, I was looking for ideas.

So consider this an idea book. I hope you'll find many things in these pages that will give you some peace and reassurance instead of one more chore.

MAN TO MAN

In Part VI, my wonderful husband, Jon Andersen, has offered an important chapter about how the journey to the altar was especially transforming for him. Not only was he deeply involved in the actual wedding day plans, he took very seriously his commitment to be spiritually prepared when that day came. Read what he has to say and share his words with your fiancé. There is no question that the invitation we extended to God to oversee our wedding became the foundation for the very happy marriage we enjoy now.

THE POWER OF WRITING IT DOWN

At the end of each chapter in this book, you will find the invitation to respond to what you have read by writing it down. Now, if you are planning a wedding, you are already writing down all sorts of things: things to remember, things to avoid, people to invite, friends to call, etc. So perhaps it would be more accurate to say that I invite you to *write it out*. There is a unique connection that is made when the heart communicates to the brain and the brain directs your hand to release the thought or emotion onto paper. What was before a vague feeling *inside* is suddenly converted to a tangible statement on the *outside*.

Writing out what you truly want for your wedding, what your dreams are, what your fears are, what your goals are, will get them out of your head and onto a piece of paper where they will either look right or wrong to you. Remember, this is not your precious wedding book in which you'll want to carefully inscribe every page with golden memories. Don't think, just write. Scribble even. But be honest with yourself.

THE POWER OF SAYING IT OUT LOUD

In the beginning was the Word. In the Bible, everything God made, He spoke into existence. He didn't think it or read it into existence. I believe there is fabric and substance to thought once it is sent out into the world in the form of sounds propelled by human energy and inhabited by your unique spirit. Don't underestimate the power of the spoken word. It is a very different experience from simply reading the words. When we speak out loud to God, we do it as an act of faith, as Abraham did, trusting that it makes a difference to "call those things that be not as though they were."

That is why, when you come across the prayer suggestions and the scripture passages in this book, I strongly encourage you to *say them out loud!* And, you will also find yourself becoming a better listener, more inclined to hear God's voice in response.

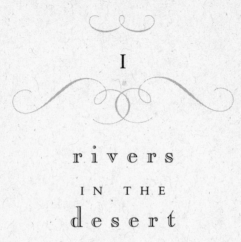

I

rivers

IN THE

desert

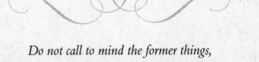

Do not call to mind the former things,
or ponder the things of the past. For behold, I will do a new thing.
Now it will spring forth. Will you not be aware of it?
I will even make a roadway in the wilderness, rivers in the desert.
ISAIAH 43:18–19

The basis of marriage is not mutual affection or feelings of emotions
and passions that we associate with love, but a vocation, a being
elected to build together a house for God in this world, to be like the
cherubs whose outstretched wings sheltered the Ark of the Covenant
and created a space where Yahweh could be present.
HENRI NOUWEN
Clowning in Rome

I BOUGHT A LOT OF WEDDING BOOKS TO INSPIRE ME AS I planned my wedding, but I didn't particularly want to wade through other people's wedding stories just to find a few good ideas. So if you decide to skip this chapter on my own wedding day saga, it won't hurt my feelings one bit. I know you're interested in making your own memories, not in imitating someone else's.

However, in the introduction I made some rather bold statements, and I challenged you to answer some very provocative questions in pursuit of a special, spiritual wedding. So I can't very well expect you to simply take my word for it, accepting that the work to be done will deliver happy results, unless I can testify that I have experienced those happy results myself.

I am not a wedding coordinator, a wedding expert, or a wedding counselor. Frankly, I don't think anything qualifies me to write this book, except my genuine passion for the subject and my sincere desire to share what I learned. I do hope this book will help you avoid making some of the mistakes I made and, ideally, that it will add to and perhaps multiply your joy.

I remember the words of Kahlil Gibran in *The Prophet*:

> *The deeper that sorrow carves into your heart,*
> *the more joy you can contain.*

I've had a lot of sorrow (mostly self-inflicted) in my romantic life. There was a point when I gave up the dream of a trusting relationship and a loving marriage altogether. I often found myself in bad relationships where I was not only getting hurt, but other people were getting hurt, too. You know you're in a bad situation when you are withdrawing from friends and relatives who might not approve of what you're doing. Chances are that at those times, you're withdrawing from God as well because you are subconsciously afraid of judgment.

But that's when we need God the most. I find most people in the process of rejecting Him have already rejected themselves. They've already decided that God is going to judge their lifestyle, their choices, and their mistakes. So many people think that if they haven't lived the perfect lifestyle, had the chaste courtship, or the breezy, uncomplicated romance, then they don't deserve God's blessing in their marriage. The truth is, as our own pastor told us, very few people go to the altar these days without regrets. But the good news is that God holds the future, as well as the past, and He doesn't give us what we deserve. As we ask Him for forgiveness, He gives us what we need. That is called grace. And that is the gift He brought to our wedding.

The first words spoken at our wedding were: "Do not call to mind the former things or ponder the things of the past. For behold, I will do a new thing!"

As those words of hope from the Book of Isaiah rang out, God *did* do something new and miraculous: Two became one. Two people with a past became one with a future. It was a long road getting there. But it was worth it.

LAYING A FOUNDATION

If marriage, at its best, is a precious thing born on your wedding day, blessed by God, protected by your vows, and nurtured to become a glorious temple for the Almighty, then, up to this point, Jon and I were only qualified to build a lean-to.

It may surprise you to hear that two people responsible for producing a television show like *Touched By An Angel* were not living in a constant spiritual state. But I believe that the privilege of creating a message of love, hope, and forgiveness every week was God's way of bringing healing to two very damaged souls. Jon was coming out of a failed marriage, and I was trying to recover from another demoralizing experience with another Mr. Wrong. So when we met at CBS Television City to discuss making a series about angels, we were absolutely not interested in falling in love. Rather, we fell into work. We learned early a lot of things that some couples only learn after marriage because we saw each other for ten, fifteen, twenty hours a day. We saw each other angry, impatient, fearful, exhausted. We learned to argue, to compromise, to support each other, and to listen to each other, because we had something besides ourselves to protect. We had something very special called *Touched By An Angel*. And, like the cherubs mentioned in the Nouwen quotation, the two of us formed a canopy of love and protection over this remarkable project, this robust television miracle that had been born so fragile and weak.

When we finally fell in love and decided to marry, Jon and I realized that we had to approach our marriage as another vocation, another project that needed to be built by and for God. And we knew we had to trust Him to help us lay a solid foundation.

This is not a "Christian" book, although we are Christians. I am terribly aware that my attempts to emulate the life of Jesus have fallen woefully short of His example. I am also aware, however, that I am a child of the One who created me and every time I take a wrong turn, His mercy and understanding always bring me back. It is a great comfort to me, being known and loved anyway. I think that's why God puts such a great value on marriage, because it can be the best example on earth of His own love for us—unconditional, intimate, and forgiving.

Unconditional love, however, can be intimidating if you don't feel you deserve it. That's also why so many people feel uncomfortable inviting God to their wedding.

But here's the good news: It's never too late to get things straight with God. And the weeks before your wedding are the best time of all.

> *When you are in distress and all these things have*
> *come upon you, in the latter days you will return to*
> *the Lord your God and listen to His Voice.*
>
> DEUTERONOMY 4:30

This book is full of opinions. I've spent the first forty-four years of my life forming opinions because those years were also spent making some incredible mistakes. When I decided to turn my life over to God, I still managed to run back, grab my life out of His hands, and come up with even more awful choices. Nevertheless, when hope ran out, when self-esteem ran out, when the men ran out, God still stuck with me. And so I pass along to you in this book some rather strong opinions about weddings and love and sex and God that I feel very passionate about—not because I did it all right, but because I did so much of it wrong.

And then God restored it.

You see, Jon and I truly wanted to start our lives over together, but we didn't know how. So we went, very humbly, to God and prayed. We laid out the whole complicated history of our lives and loves. We asked Him to do whatever was necessary to prepare us for our wedding and for our marriage. It wasn't easy or fast, but over the months, God created in me and in Jon a new heart. And I walked down the aisle feeling restored and reborn. Ready to begin a brand new life. All the old things had passed away, and everything was new again. That is what I hope you will feel on your wedding day.

THREE REVELATIONS

There is a photograph of me from my wedding that always comes to mind whenever someone asks, "What were you thinking on your wedding day?" It is not the most flattering picture, but I love it because I remember exactly what I was thinking when that picture was taken. It was moments before I was to walk down the aisle, and in those moments I believe that God sent me a message in three separate and distinct revelations. This message was about myself and my life, and it gave me peace about my past and allowed me to step into the sanctuary with confidence and utter joy.

THE MESSAGE OF FRIENDSHIP

In the photograph I am peeking through the drapes that separate me and my bridesmaids from the "sanctuary," where friends on the other side are watching the choir perform before the ceremony. Over my shoulder, watching along with me, is my dear friend Gwen, a brilliant oncologist and researcher who is not often seen in velvet and tulle. Gwen and I became best college friends when we discovered that we both shared a love of music and an unusual ability to harmonize and sing together without a trace of the competitive attitude that women in music often have. Years earlier I had the honor of singing at her wedding, and, after she preceded me down the aisle, she would sing at mine.

But now we were standing "backstage" watching the ceremony begin, waiting for our cue. It was an awesome moment of realization that on the other side of that curtain sat all the people who mattered most to me. I was watching them watch the wedding I had thought would never come. And I knew that more than a few of the people in those pews had thought the same thing. But the day was here. The hour was now.

The bagpiper played the simple strains of "Jesus loves me, this I know, for the Bible tells me so," and I recalled that I was once a little girl who dreamed of a big, happy wedding. Friends from high school and college and church walked down the aisle and took their seats in the choir loft, and I silently thanked God for the inexpressible blessings of friends who have loved me, known me, forgiven me, and always been there for me and who were here once again to stand up and sing for me today.

THE MESSAGE OF HEALING

Gwen and I kept peeking through the curtain, our heads pressed together. When an usher blocked our view, I poked him in the back. He jumped, surprised to discover the bride waving at him through the folds of the tent! He stepped aside just in time for me to see Jon's childhood friend, Stacy Keach, step to the podium and read my favorite chapter from the Bible, Isaiah 58. It was a song of hope for me at my lowest point in life when I couldn't imagine a happy day like this. Lonely, single, without much of a career at thirty, I felt damaged in heart and mind and spirit. The little girl who had big dreams of doing something that mattered in the world had almost given up on life itself. And then I found this promise in Isaiah:

Then your light shall break forth like the morning, your
healing shall spring forth . . . your light shall dawn in

darkness and your darkness shall be as the noonday. The
Lord will continually guide you and satisfy your soul in
dry places and strengthen your bones. You shall be like a
watered garden and like a spring of water whose waters do
not fail . . . you shall be called the repairer of the breach,
the restorer of the streets in which to dwell.

There it all was, in one piece of scripture: a promise of healing, of productivity, and of purpose. At the end of every
Touched By An Angel episode, there appears the logo of my production company MoonWater Productions. The name came
from these words in Isaiah that Stacy was now reading. Moon-
Water was a private reference to the promise that God had
kept—there would be light in the darkness and an overflowing
of blessings that would be new every morning. It all came true,
and to be reminded of it only moments before I walked down
the aisle was a deeply private and moving moment that I shared
with the Father.

THE MESSAGE OF FAMILY

My sister Mary Lou stood to read my favorite passage of love
and loyalty:

Entreat me not to leave you, or to turn back from following
you. For wherever you go, I shall go. And wherever you
lodge, I shall lodge. Your people shall be my people and
your God, my God. Where you die, I will die, and there
will I be buried. The Lord do so to me and more also if
ought but death parts thee and me.

RUTH 1:16–17

It is a beautiful vow of commitment, and my sister's voice cracked as she read the words. In that moment I felt a rush of love for her. Until then, everything had gone so completely according to the "script" I had written. But Mary Lou's emotional reading suddenly charged the room with an energy that never left. Her tears and sweet smile reminded us all that something precious was happening here.

Gwen squeezed my hand as I prepared to see my mother take the microphone and begin to sing "The Lord's Prayer." It would be the last thing before the Wedding March and the procession of bride and bridesmaids. But my mother didn't move. Instead, my sister Peggy was standing up and preparing to sing. A glitch! The bridal plans were being seriously altered! Every bone in my producer's body went on alert. My mind was racing, but there was nothing I could do. I couldn't yell, "Cut!" For the first time in my life, I realized that, as we say in show business, "the ship has sailed." There was nothing to do but watch what was going to happen next.

The pianist played the introduction and Peggy, an alto, began to sing the soprano solo. "Our Father which art in heaven . . ."

I realized that something must have happened to Mother. Later I learned that the overwhelming events of the day had just moved her eighty-one-year-old heart so much that she couldn't sing without breaking down. We Williamsons are a sentimental bunch and make no excuse for the Irish side of Mother's family. We alternately weep with great passion and pride. And when one can't go any longer, another family member picks right up where the other left off.

And that's what happened. My mother gave Peggy a look, Peggy jumped up and started to sing. My other sister, Mary Lou, sat in the choir watching Peggy's every breath, practically willing her to reach that last high note: "For Thine is the kingdom and the power and the glory for-eeev-ver!" Peggy had landed squarely on the note and survived stunningly. Mary Lou and my mother beamed. Peggy blew my mother a kiss and took her seat. In that moment I saw the history and custom of our family: "The show must go on. Never let the flag hit the ground." I had to laugh. It was the Lord's last message to me before I began my new life: "Look at what a wonderful family you have. Your mother loves you so much she can't even express it right now; your sisters will do anything to support you and your dream; and your father is sitting up here with Me in heaven chuckling at 'his girls.'" It was the last memory I have as a single woman.

A STEP IN THE RIGHT DIRECTION

I have seen many brides walk down the aisle. I am always amazed by the ones who don't seem all that happy about it. They look straight ahead, their eyes fixed on some distant point, as if they are models on a runway, allowing themselves to be viewed and evaluated. Chances are, of course, that they are simply too nervous to think about anything but getting to the altar without passing out. Gwen, the doctor, once had to leave her seat and prescribe Compazine for a bride who had gotten herself into such a state that she had been vomiting for three hours before the wedding.

I vowed to myself that when I got married someday, no matter what illness or accident befell me, I would have a great big smile on my face when my feet hit that long white runner.

As it turned out, it was the easiest thing in the world. The music soared, and my bridesmaids began disappearing through

17

the door. I grabbed the arm of Don Fuchs, my surrogate dad and father of my college pal Betsy. We turned the corner, stepped through the chapel doors, and began the walk. I'd give anything to live that over just once more.

Some people have called it "the longest walk." For me, it was far too short. I wish we had casually strolled down that aisle so that I could have permanently recorded every joyful instant. Instead, as most brides will tell you, it was all one surrealistic blur. Only impressions remain, mixed up now with images from the videotape. But there are three pure moments of my very own that I can still conjure in my memory:

THIS IS IT

First, the shock of realizing that everyone is standing there, waiting for you, and this is *it*. The years of practicing writing "Mr. and Mrs." on the inside covers of algebra books and three-ring binders were over. The twenty-year subscription to *Bride's Magazine* could now be canceled. The dream was coming true. And strangely enough, perhaps even more jolting, was the realization that my long-held dream would itself be a memory in a matter of hours. And so, I was beaming as I walked down the aisle. But I dragged my feet a little, too.

THE REASON TO GET TO THE END
OF THE AISLE

The second indelible memory that I cherish is the instant I realized that as much as I was enjoying this promenade past my friends and family, delighted to see their faces and the love they were trying to send me with their eyes, there was also a very good reason to get to the end of the aisle. My darling Jon was waiting for me there. One of the greatest gifts that God bestowed upon me that day was realizing that despite the fact that almost everyone I've ever truly loved was in that room at that moment, I was only looking for one face. I wanted to get to that altar just to see the man I'd been searching for all my life.

Sitting in the choir was a good friend and a woman of great faith, Ruthie. Whenever we would get together and commiserate about men, her eyes would twinkle and she'd say, humorously but with great conviction, "Martha, God is making just the right man for you. He's in the oven somewhere baking. But he's not ready yet! So don't ask God to take him out until your man is done!" Well, as silly as that sounds, something had always told me that Ruthie was right. I had made a few misbegotten steps toward the altar in my life, but I always knew that the recipe was off and the match was wrong. Now, here I was at the end of the road, at the end of the aisle, facing the man I believed God had created for me. And it felt right.

I have actually spoken to people who have admitted they knew even as they stood at the altar that they were making a mistake. Others have simply obsessed, and confessed later that as much as they love and adore their husbands, there was the briefest of moments at the altar when he looked like a complete stranger. But that is nothing to second-guess yourself about. There *is* an instant, a split second when you may look at your husband-to-be and you are hit by the sheer enormity of what you are about to do and you ask yourself, "How did I get here?" But that isn't indecision. That is one of the purest moments I think a woman can feel. It is the absolute realization that until this very moment, she was alone. And in the next moments, she will *choose* to merge her life with that of another human being. It's a powerful and sobering discovery; in half a second, you will see him with great clarity as almost a stranger, an unfamiliar fellow, mortal and fallible, whom you have probably not even known as long as your bridesmaids. But with the other half of that second comes the amazing thing: You love him. You can't imagine going another day without him in your life.

Years ago someone gave me the advice "Don't marry anyone unless you can't imagine living without him." It was during the aggressively feminist seventies and I recall deciding that I could never allow a man to become that important to me. A partner, perhaps. A fellow traveler on the road, certainly. But a lifeline? Forget it. And I did forget it. I worked tremendously hard for years proving that I was an independent individual who didn't need anyone. And it worked.

But then I met Jon. Our association could be best described as "constructive"; I was the architect and he was the engineer. He literally made my dreams come true on the screen. He respected my talent; he embraced my crazy vision of angels with attitudes who talked sincerely about God on television. He supported me and protected me, and most important, he just plain liked me. And I liked him.

It wasn't love at first sight. It was just hard work almost twenty-four hours a day. The first years of the series were so demanding that I often fell asleep on the couch in my office and woke up only to brush my teeth in the ladies' room and start working again. It's fair to say that I was not interested in men or romance; I was interested in survival. Our dinners were about scripts and schedules. Our talks were about the vision of the show, the message of the angels. We were buddies in the trenches, fighting a war of deadlines and budgets and skepticism, exhausted and yet committed to keeping it all going. Because that was the only way we would win.

The time finally came when it seemed that we might actually have a hit. On top of that, we had another series to produce for CBS: *Promised Land*, the story of a family that traveled around America in a mobile home. The last-minute pilot was inspired by Jon's frequent, half-joking threats to quit the insanity of Hollywood and just drive across the country in an Airstream trailer. With two shows on the air, it was going to be the busiest and most challenging year ever. I would never have taken on the responsibility if I hadn't thought Jon would be there to help me see it through.

LEAVING JON AT THE ALTAR

During the hiatus between Season Two and Season Three, I realized something else. I missed him. Seven days before production was to begin, I went to a desert spa to eke out one last weekend of relaxation. I had spoken to Jon on the phone two days earlier. He was out of the country and casually mentioned that he wasn't feeling well. I told him not to take any chances and to go to the hospital and have himself checked out. He said he'd think about it. Just like a guy.

Two days later I was having the best massage of my life, two hours of deep-muscle work and hot towels and aromatherapy. More of a healing than a massage. I was truly floating in another dimension. A siren could have gone off by my ear and I wouldn't have heard it. And yet I did hear something.

I believe that when God speaks to you, it is with a very still, small voice. It says so in the Bible, in 1 Kings 19:12, and it's been

my experience as well. It is a thought, a "knowing," an awareness that starts in your heart before it ever hits your mind. That
is how I recognize when God's Spirit touches me. There is a lot
of wishful thinking that is attributed to God, but in fact, that's
all it is—thinking. The wish starts in your head and makes its
way down to your heart and before you know it, you've convinced yourself that this is God's will because *you* willed your
thought into an emotion. But I don't think any word that has
ever come from God's Spirit to me was emotional. It's just
something deep within me that is simply there and true and it
wasn't there before.

And that's what happened during that massage. I was relaxed
and perhaps more open to hear that "still, small voice." In one
instant, I was wide awake and urgently aware that I needed to
begin praising God and thanking Him for Jon's life.

Even more imperative was the sense that I needed to release
my reliance on him and the protection and support that he gave
me, and turn him over to God. It meant that Jon, my "secret
weapon" and a key to my own success, belonged to God and
not to me. I would have to trust God to get me through the next
season, not Jon, not myself, not any human at all.

The greatest, and perhaps most misunderstood lesson of
trust in God can be found in the story of Abraham. Burnt offer-
ings and blood sacrifices were part of the Hebrew culture. The
practice of offering your best to God, giving Him the first fruits
of your labor, was a basic principle of the faith. Much is made of
the "cruelty" of God's testing of Abraham. How could God ask
a man to place his own son on the altar and kill him? I personally believe that God was not testing Abraham in the pass-or-fail
context in which we test each other today. I believe that God
never asks us to do anything that will ultimately harm us. In fact,

the more difficult the task He has placed before me, the stronger I have always become.

The idea of "giving up Jon" and placing him on God's altar was incredibly hard to do. I didn't know why, but right there in the middle of the massage, I opened my eyes, looked at the therapist, and said, "I hope you don't mind, but I'm supposed to pray right now." She smiled and said, "Go right ahead. I'll pray with you."

And so I prayed a prayer of thanks for Jon. I told God that Jon belonged to Him, not to me. And that whatever God's plans for Jon, I had no claim on him. I simply wanted Jon to be well and happy wherever the Lord decided to put him next.

A PRAYER ANSWERED

Three days later I received a call from a mutual friend and learned that Jon was hospitalized in a tiny community hospital near his home. He'd had peritonitis and miraculously, in an underfunded, understaffed, ancient medical facility, there had been one nearly retired surgeon who knew how to perform an emergency surgery that saved Jon's life. I realized that at the same time I had been praying for Jon during my massage, he had been receiving last rites from an Anglican priest a thousand miles away.

Despite the surgery, Jon was still not out of danger, and there were many times over the next weeks when I went back to the altar. It was there that I had put him in God's hands, and I knew that only by God's will and not my own would I see Jon again. The act of releasing Jon to God's care and purpose was not something I wanted to do at all. I think the job of executive producer was invented for control freaks like me who need a twenty-four-hour expression of their condition!

But God knows that. And I believe He knew even then that if I could give up some control for once in my life, if I could just find peace in the obedient act without having an acceptable explanation first, if I could simply trust God's plan instead of my own, then I would meet Jon at the altar someday. But according to God's rules, not mine.

During Jon's recovery, I had to hold down the fort on the two television series being shot in Utah. It was a lonely, lonely time. Not until he was absent did I realize how much I counted on him, not just to keep the production going but to keep me going, too.

And, of course, I realized that I was in love with him.

I won't venture to guess when Jon actually realized he was in love with me. But I do know that we both see that separation as a turning point. Not just in our relationship with each other, but in our individual relationships with God. Little did we know at the time that God was using the first of many forms of separation to prepare us for a marriage.

THE LONG-DISTANCE OPERATOR

One of my favorite episodes of "Touched" was titled "The Spirit of Liberty Moon." It told the story of a young Chinese woman in the United States who had fled Beijing after her participation in the Tiananmen Square protests. Forced to leave her little girl behind in China, she often gazed at the moon and recalled that she had taught her child, Liberty Moon, to do the same thing. It gave her comfort and a sense of connection to look up at night and see the moon, knowing that somewhere her daughter was looking at it, too.

That moment in the script was inspired by the unusual connection I had with Jon during those weeks of separation. We not only had the moon in common, but we both now shared a new experience of God. God was now running this relationship, relaying a peaceful connection between me and Jon like a long-distance operator. And, like the moon, there was now a sort of spiritual meeting place for all three of us, the space that God was starting to carve out for us where our marriage would eventually live.

REUNITED

Jon's near-death experience had changed us both. My faith had been tested and increased. Jon's faith had been revived when he himself was revived in a recovery room. In those days of great pain, Jon realized that nothing, not money, not prestige, not a hit show, not even love could save his life. He had only one course of action—to appeal to the Almighty for help. And when he received it, he did not forget. He began to study the Bible and to seek the counsel of men of faith whom he respected.

It is interesting to me that as he lay on that gurney, Jon never tried to "bargain" with God. I always find it amazing that people who attempt deathbed deals actually think they have something that the Creator of the Universe could use. It is most pleasing to God, I believe, when we simply throw ourselves on His mercy and say, "Help!" It's admitting our helplessness that gets us out of God's way so that He can really make a difference. I did that on the massage table; Jon did that on the operating table. And God went to work.

I will never forget the day that Jon returned to Salt Lake City. He was weak and thin and clearly still not well. I met him at the airport. Or rather, I hid behind a column and peeked around it, watching for him to get off the plane. He had warned me that he didn't look good, and I wanted to prepare myself and get any trace of shock off my face before he spotted me.

He walked off the plane and onto the concourse and looked around hesitantly. Man, did he look terrible!

And wonderful.

I stepped out from behind the post and waved to him. His face lit up and we walked toward each other with tears in our eyes.

Every love story is different. And yet I believe that every love story can be told only one way or the other: "There were two people who did the best they could to love each other, drawing on their own strength and their own experience and their own intelligence." Or: "There were two people who asked God to create a place for them where their love could exist and be nurtured and protected by Him, even in the times when they were unable to sustain it themselves."

I believe that God creates these spaces of peace where the love of two people can be placed in a kind of "trust" that becomes, in fact, a third entity in the relationship. The room where two individuals meet to share their love. Where love only accumulates and never leaves. There is peace, there is God, and there is an altar. That altar is where we pray, where we worship, and where we lay down our burdens.

And now, whenever Jon and I are apart, it is the place I go to. It is the meeting place where God and I and Jon meet, no matter how many miles divide us. And it will be the place where we shall meet when death parts us.

THROUGH THE LOOKING GLASS

And so on my wedding day, as I walked the last steps down the aisle, I recalled the trials and the tears and the hard spiritual work we had gone through to feel that we had a right to be married in God's presence. As I stepped up to the altar, I remembered the day I had placed Jon on another altar and into God's hands. Now, here he was, waiting for me there.

And so that's why the half a second as you arrive at the altar, when you say, "How did I get here?" is such a blessing. Because how you got there made all the difference. You see your fiancé as the individual he is and yet as an undeniable part of you. That joy, of finding your mate in the other half of that eternal second, is like stepping through the looking glass. Once you do, you realize you've been on the wrong side of the mirror all along.

On that day, and for every day since, whenever I turn a corner or walk into a room and see my husband standing there, I still get that same thrill. And I still see my happiest, most beautiful self in his eyes. It may sound sappy, but hey, that's love.

THE PRESENCE OF GOD

The third and most powerful of memories as I walked down the aisle is the palpable sense of the presence of God in that space. As we'd prepared for the wedding, once again, I had been the architect, and Jon had been the engineer. He directed the tent building and lighting. I wrote the "play-by-play" for the musicians, the bridesmaids, the choir, etc. We had wanted to be married in a small church in Santa Barbara near the ranch where the reception would take place. Logistics finally made it clear that we would have to be married on the ranch property. This would certainly make it easier to move 150 people from ceremony to dinner; all they had to do was walk. But I was disappointed; there was no church. And then I remembered a worship song I had always loved, "Surely the Presence (of the Lord Is in This Place)." Hadn't we sung that song in classrooms? In private homes? In the car? Surely the presence of God was wherever God was. And so we built a "church" of canvas and iron fence and stained glass and borrowed church pews. And we simply decided to ask God to "hallow the ground" by inviting His presence on that spot before the ceremony began.

I didn't plan it this way, but the scriptures and music that preceded the procession of the bride actually shifted the focus of the evening off of Jon and me and created instead an evening of worship in which a sacred union took place.

We had chosen scriptures and music that not only meant a great deal to me and Jon, but glorified God as well. In the Book of Psalms, the Bible says that "God inhabits the praises of His people." And I'd learned early in my spiritual life to begin my prayers with praise and thanksgiving. Something undeniably supernatural takes place when you praise God with words and music, as if the door to heaven opens and glory fills the room, the closet, the car. Praise is a natural invitation to God, and wherever it takes place, God knows He is welcome there, and He shows up.

And so as the music played and the praise began, the winds blew, the rains came down, the tent shook violently sometimes, and the candles threatened to topple and set the whole thing on fire. There was a sense of drama throughout the whole wedding ceremony. But greater than that was the very real sense of the presence of the Lord. We had many guests who attended our wedding who did not share our faith, but nevertheless said they were inspired and deeply moved by what they called "the spirit in the room." Everyone felt like a participant in a miracle. And the miracles happened. The rain stopped. An honest-to-goodness double rainbow arched over the valley, and two people became one.

ideas to ponder

DON'T DWELL ON THE MISTAKES YOU'VE made. Rejoice instead in all the miracles that it took for you and your fiancé to find each other.

As a tribute to my father, we included in the service one of his favorite hymns, "Great Is Thy Faithfulness." In the song are the wonderful words of comfort "morning by morning new mercies I see." And it's true that no matter what has come before, God brings a whole new day of mercy every time the sun rises. He must have known that we would all need it.

write it out

SO MANY BRIDES KNOW WHAT THEY WANT TO *do* on their wedding day and what they want to *look like* on their wedding day. But how do you want to *feel*? Years from now when you remember that day, what are the words you hope to use then to describe yourself as you walked down the aisle? Relaxed? Peaceful? Confident? Write them down.

Confident
Covenental
Excited
Overjoyed

If God gave you three messages to remind you of His blessings in your life, what would they be?

- Trust in Him + you shall Receive in abundance
- Do everything in /with LOVE
- Just look around you at everything He has done

say it out loud

THIS IS A BOOK ABOUT INVITING GOD TO help you plan your wedding, and if He's going to show up, you need to let Him know that you have faith in His ability to make a difference. But "faith comes by hearing, and hearing by the word of God" (Romans 10:17). So, start hearing yourself say what you believe *out loud*. Let's begin with a simple scripture that has always been an encouragement to me: "With God, all things are possible." Go ahead, say it out loud! "With God, all things are possible!" Okay, you've said it. And before this book is finished, it's my sincere hope that you'll believe it.

II

preparing
spiritually
FOR YOUR
wedding

Unless the Lord builds the house,
those who build it labor in vain.
PSALM 127:1

the first
invitation
goes to God

You COULD GET MARRIED IN THREE MINUTES IN front of two witnesses and someone with the authority to declare you legally married. You don't need a cake, you don't need champagne, you don't need a room full of spectators, and you don't need music or even a wedding dress.

You probably need a license and, of course, someone who wants to spend the rest of his life with you. That's important. I begin this book with the assumption that you are actually marrying someone for that reason—that you both are madly in love and can't imagine living life without each other.

But you are also reading this book because you're interested in having Someone Else at the wedding. At some level you understand that a wedding between two people, an officiant, and two or even two hundred witnesses is certainly legal, possibly romantic, and definitely optimistic, but it isn't necessarily a spiritual event. However, if God attends your wedding, you are replacing optimism with faith and genuine hope. You are saying that you are aware of the challenges that marriage presents and

INVITING GOD TO YOUR WEDDING

that you are asking God to be there with you both at the very beginning and to stay with you on the journey until death do you part.

> *There is a ship and it sails the sea . . .*
> *Give us a boat that can carry two*
> *And both shall row, my love and I.*

Marriage is not so much an institution as it is a conveyance, and I often think of these lyrics from a folk song when I try to describe marriage as a form of transportation through life. However, "Unless the Lord builds the house," or in this case the ship, "we labor in vain," says the Bible (Psalm 127:1). The time to construct the boat is not when it's in the middle of troubled waters. It makes the most sense to build it in fair weather before it ever has to ride out a storm. That's why it's good to invite God from the very beginning, to help you design your ship and set your course. That means that a spiritual marriage begins with a spiritual wedding. And a spiritual wedding begins with spiritual preparation. It's not just about picking hymns and choosing readings from the Bible. It's about preparing your own heart to be as emotionally and spiritually ready as possible to step into that boat when the big day comes!

And so, the first wedding invitation that you send should be a very personal one, a prayer that asks God to attend not only the ceremony on your wedding day, but to be there for all the decisions and the details beforehand. Remember, God holds time in His hands. Whatever concerns you have about the months to come, He is already there in the future and He can give you peace about it. So it is perfectly right and appropriate to include Him today. Don't wait until the morning of your wedding to ask Him to show up. There is so much He can do right now to help.

I know, it's hard to imagine. Why would God care about your wedding? People make the mistake of assuming that God is too busy with "really important issues" to be bothered with somebody's nuptials. But that was never my experience. I love this line from a popular hymn that I sing to myself whenever I think my needs are too trivial for God.

His eye is on the sparrow and I know He watches me.

His eye is on you, too. And I know He is watching and waiting for your invitation.

ideas to ponder

THE GREEKS DESCRIBED LOVE IN THREE forms. The first two are "Eros" and "Philia." Eros is the love that expresses itself romantically. Philia is friendship. H. Norman Wright describes the two this way: "While eros is almost always a face-to-face relationship, philia is often a shoulder-to-shoulder relationship." Finally, the third form of love is "Agape"—the love that is unconditional and asks nothing in return. That is, perhaps, the best love of all. Beyond face-to-face and shoulder-to-shoulder, there must be heart-to-heart. When you marry "for love," are all forms of it present in your relationship? As you prepare spiritually for your wedding, ask God to bring all three into balance.

write it out

YOUR FIRST WEDDING INVITATION IS GOING OUT
to God. Before you invite Him, however, be clear on
the reasons you want Him there. Write them down.

_____

_____

_____

_____

_____

_____

_____

_____

_____

_____

_____

_____

_____

_____

say it out loud

Call to Me and I will answer you.
And I will tell you great and mighty things which you
do not know.

JEREMIAH 33:3

GOD WANTS TO ATTEND YOUR WEDDING, BUT HE won't go if He's not invited. Take a private moment to ask, out loud, for God's presence not only at your wedding but throughout the planning process.

Dear God,

Even with all the friends and loved ones I have who want to help me, I need Someone who will really make the difference between a ceremony and a miracle. Will You help me? Will You teach me and my fiancé how to truly become one? I believe You will. Thank You.

Amen.

2

wait a minute,
I feel like a
hypocrite!

O Lord, You have searched me
and known me. You know when
I sit down and when I rise up;
You understand my thoughts from afar.
You scrutinize my path and my lying
down, and are intimately acquainted
with my ways.

PSALM 139:1–3

JUST BECAUSE YOU'RE READING THIS BOOK, I CANNOT assume that you have a strong, ongoing relationship with God. In fact, I'm hoping that there are some people who have decided to read this before their wedding because they sense instinctively that they have very real issues of faith that need to be resolved before they get married. There is nothing like considering your vows, for instance, to force you to confront your beliefs. It's natural to say, "God bless you," when someone sneezes. It's easy to say, "God help me," when you run a red light and to utter a relieved "thank God" when you don't see a police car flashing its lights in the rearview mirror. But when someone says, "Dearly beloved, we are gathered here today in the sight of God . . ." or "What God has joined together, let no man put asunder," you have to decide what you really believe about God.

So many of us are tempted to believe that we don't deserve to ask God to our wedding or into our lives at all until we're "presentable." I know some people who, as much as they wanted a spiritual wedding, felt embarrassed about the circumstances that brought them to the altar and didn't feel they had the right to invite God to meet them there. Or, they'd been so distant from God for so long that they were afraid He would consider it hypocritical to remember Him now.

It reminds me of when I was a little girl and my mother and my father worked long hours together in the office. There was not much time left at the end of the day for dusting and vacuuming and other domestic chores. So my father convinced my mother to hire a housekeeper to clean the house on Fridays. It became a family joke that Thursday nights Mother would run around the house, cleaning everything up before Ellen, the housekeeper, came because she didn't want Ellen to think we were messy!

THE PRODIGAL BRIDE

Perhaps it's been a long time since you've prayed or been to church or truly shared a quiet moment with your Creator. And if so, you may feel awkward about inviting God to your wedding. But don't. Don't waste time trying to "clean up your house" before inviting God inside. He'll meet you anytime, no matter where you are in your faith.

Maybe you attend worship services regularly. Maybe you only go to church or synagogue on holidays. Maybe you don't attend anything at all and you "find God" on the ski slope or the beach on your Sabbath day. Maybe you read the Bible every day and consider it your "handbook for life," or perhaps the last time you read the Bible was in a hotel room on a lonely night. Everyone is in a different place spiritually. But God knows that. If you ask Him to help, that's not hypocrisy. That's courage.

But the fact remains, you don't want to invite a stranger to your wedding, so if you're interested in inviting God to yours, it's a good idea to actually get to know Him better. There is one very simple way to begin that relationship: Decide that you want it and then tell Him.

> *Draw nigh unto God and He*
> *will draw nigh unto you.*
>
> JAMES 4:8

If you already have a relationship with God, let this be the moment when you pray for a deeper, richer knowledge of Him.

ideas to ponder

All I have seen teaches me to trust the
Creator for all I have not seen.
RALPH WALDO EMERSON

THERE IS A STORY A RABBI TOLD EIGHT HUN-
dred years ago. If a thousand angels reported to
God about you but only one angel among them
had anything good to say, that is the angel God
would listen to. It is a beautiful example of God's
love for us and His eternal desire that we should
come to Him anytime, no matter how long
we've been away.

write it out

SO MANY OF US TRY TO "CLEAN OUR HOUSE" before we feel ready to invite God into it. But God is a "House Cleaner." Is there anything in your life you would like Him to help sweep away before you get married?

_____

_____

_____

_____

_____

_____

_____

_____

_____

_____

_____

_____

_____

_____

say it out loud

Now, take this opportunity to hand the key to your house over to God:

Dear God,

It's an incredible and humbling thought to imagine that You know all about me. Sometimes I feel I don't even have the right to come to You and ask for anything. But since You know me, I believe You also know what I need and what I need to change even better than I do. So, I'm handing You the key to my heart. It is a messy home that needs straightening up before I get married. Prepare in me a clean heart, O Lord, and renew a right spirit in me. I believe You will. Thank You.

Amen.

3

I don't want a "religious" wedding

It is a mistake to suppose that God is only, or even chiefly, concerned with religion.
ARCHBISHOP WILLIAM TEMPLE

DON'T CONFUSE A RELIGIOUS WEDDING WITH A GOD-is-present wedding. God doesn't need to be *inserted* into your ceremony if He's already been invited. And I believe, therefore, that you will find natural ways to include Him, and He will make His presence known as long as you open the door.

There can be something very beautiful and comforting about ritual and ceremony. A candle lit in memory of a loved one, the tying of a knot, or the breaking of a glass at a wedding: All of these and other rituals are sacred and have profound religious meaning. But there's always the danger of oft-repeated ritual becoming "ordinary" and replacing true worship and celebration. Guard against your ceremony becoming just a formality. Our pastor addressed this at the beginning of our celebration:

There's a tremendous tendency for anything that smacks of ritual to become merely that—a rote performance.

It's true. I have often sat in a pew watching a wedding that was beautiful and "religious," and yet I somehow felt something was missing. Many times I felt "left out" of a wedding because I didn't understand the rituals taking place, or worse, because it was clear the bride and groom didn't understand them either. They seemed to be "going through the motions" of a wedding—saying the words, giving the rings—but they were not really aware of the tradition of worship that was being celebrated. Depending on your particular faith, you will probably want to include readings from the Scriptures as well as hymns and prayers in your wedding ceremony. But the ceremony doesn't have to be so "religious" that it becomes remote and sanctimonious.

You want your guests to feel included no matter what their beliefs are. You want them to be moved by the miracle of your love for one another and by the miracle of two becoming one. You also want them to participate spiritually. And you might be surprised that they want to participate, too.

Jon and I were married in a Christian ceremony, and I wanted to hear hymns we've loved since childhood and Bible verses that have had transforming meaning for both of us. The elements of our Christian ceremony had the potential to alienate and perhaps even offend some of our non-Christian guests. We certainly didn't want that, but we didn't want to compromise the sacredness of the ceremony and its meaning for us. We discussed these concerns with our minister, Jack Hayford, and his wife, Anna, the wise and remarkable couple that faithfully pastored The Church On The Way in Southern California for over thirty years. Pastor Hayford has sensitively performed many unapologetically Christian weddings where numerous "nonbelievers" attended. This is what he said to our guests:

> I'd like to invite you to become more than a spectator. Become a participant, and let these moments that have a lot of emotional warmth (because of our care for Jon and Martha) become moments when we open up to an element of the miraculous, and I mean that sincerely. The Bible records the presence of Jesus at one wedding we know of, and it's the wedding that is marked by the miracle of the water being turned to wine. He is still in the business of doing the same thing, but it's not a water-to-wine miracle so much as it is the ordinary to the extraordinary. Our humanness needs to be touched by divine grace in order for the beauty of a wonderful marriage to occur. And that requires a miracle. And in this moment, I believe we can all open our hearts to a miracle, not just praying for Jon and Martha, but for ourselves, saying "Lord, do something of Your grace in my heart while I'm here, too."

Many of the people who were at my wedding have told me that they accepted the invitation to participate, and that the experience was extremely powerful. They weren't just sitting there watching. Some people, sitting with their spouses of many years, said they felt a sense of renewal in their own relationships. Other people, whether single or married, prayed about their personal needs and received comfort.

So let your wedding reflect your beliefs and those of your fiancé, but add an inclusive element that takes the ceremony out of the realm of a rote performance. Don't let your "religious" ceremony become a yawner to sit through before the fun begins at the reception. Why not make your ceremony a meaningful and memorable occasion for all concerned? After all, if you've invited God to your wedding, you might want to encourage others to receive the benefit of His presence.

ideas to ponder

DON'T LIMIT GOD TO JUST THE PART OF your life that's "religious." Imagine a pie in which the slices are various aspects of who you are— your job, your fiancé, your family, your friends, your hobbies, your dreams, and your goals.

Now, God is not one of those slices of your pie. He is the whole pie plate. He is the One who pulls the whole thing together and keeps it all from falling apart. He is with you if you attend services in a house of worship. But if you invite Him into your life, He is also with you at the office and on the tennis court and in the kitchen.

Remember that your wedding might be the first time in a long time that some of your guests have even thought about God, and they might feel uncomfortable because they have unfinished business with Him. Pastor Hayford addressed this and got quite a laugh when he said, "Integrity doesn't come to any of us naturally. There is a desperate need for wholeness in our lives. I think it might be a bit of an exaggeration to say that we are bankrupt of character—but we are all certainly underfunded!" Acknowledging that we all could use "a little religion" at a time like this helps everyone to relax.

write it out

ALL SORTS OF THINGS COME TO MIND WHEN WE hear the word *religious*, words like *pious*, *judgmental*, *stuffy*, etc. Don't assume that a wedding that includes God necessarily has to be inaccessible and rigid. *Religious* can also mean "loyal," "devout," "committed." When friends ask, "Is it going to be a religious ceremony?" what will you say? What other words can you use besides *religious*?

_____

_____

_____

_____

_____

_____

_____

_____

_____

_____

_____

_____

_____

_____

say it out loud

Dear God,

I am not inviting You to my wedding just because I want to follow tradition, perform rituals, or "be religious." I want You there so that You can bless our union and profoundly change an "ordinary" ceremony into something "extraordinary." As we plan our wedding, make us aware of any ritual or observance that we can include to celebrate Your presence. But also reveal to us anything that is simply an exercise in religiosity. Lord, I want to get married with You actually there, not just mentioned. Please, show us how to do that.

Amen.

4

celebrating
our happiness
is celebrating God

Where the Spirit of the Lord is, there is liberty.
2 CORINTHIANS 3:17

WHEN PEOPLE LOOK AT THE PICTURES IN OUR
wedding album, they always comment on how happy everyone looks. It's true. I'm beaming. Jon is beaming. Our families
are beaming. Our friends are beaming. I have no doubt that God
was beaming, too.

There's no question that we had a "religious" ceremony with
tradition and ritual. But we also had a jubilant ceremony full of
music and personal touches. Inviting God to attend didn't mean
that we had to curtail our expressions of joy that day. In fact, His
presence there seemed to increase it.

During the ceremony there were many moments of humor
and spontaneity. There was reverence, and worship, too, but it
was far from a solemn occasion.

We invited God to the reception as well. And there we had
rock-and-roll music and big band swing dancing and even a

sing-along. At one point Jon grabbed a guitar and played the blues, even though there wasn't a blue soul to be found that night. With the help of my old cabaret partner Gwen, I sang a love song to Jon. It was called "Unexpected Song," and from the look on Jon's face, you could tell it was truly unexpected. In one special picture taken at that moment, he clasps his hand to his heart and gasps in delight as we surprise him with our number. It wasn't the best I had ever sung, but I had never sung with more love, and Jon was blessed by that.

It was a very musical night, obviously. But more than that, it was a merry one expressed in song and dance, with funny toasts and touching tributes. I specifically remember my friend Bob Colleary, who went to all the trouble of memorizing his toast to us in the Samoan language as a nod to Jon's love of the South Seas. We laughed until we cried. I can't remember an evening that was more fun.

God must have been pleased to see His children joyously celebrating their love for each other and for Him. So don't get the idea that God's presence at your wedding means you can't have a grand time. Sing and dance and celebrate to your heart's content with assurance that He'll be celebrating right along with you.

ideas to ponder

ROMA DOWNEY, THE BEAUTIFUL STAR OF *Touched By An Angel,* always looked forward to seeing me get married. She'd frequently wink and quote a saying from her native Ireland: "I'll dance at your wedding, my girl." It's a natural thing for people to want to dance and sing and rejoice at your wedding. You may not be able to have a band, but a deejay or a piano player in the background provides a wonderful accompaniment to your day. Music always speaks what the heart can't find the words to express.

write it out

MOST BRIDES EXPECT THEIR WEDDING DAY TO be the happiest of their life. But oddly enough, it's also perhaps the most unusual day of their life. What are the "usual" things that make you happy? Ice cream? Rock and roll? Balloons? Church bells? Crayons? A walk on the beach? Write down things that make you happy and joyful every day, and see which of them can be incorporated into your wedding day.

_____

_____

_____

_____

Music is an important part of the wedding. What songs would you like played during the ceremony? And during the reception? Why?

_____

_____

_____

_____

_____

say it out loud

*Shout for joy to the Lord, all the earth! Burst
into jubilant song with music; make music to
the Lord with the harp, with the harp and the
sound of singing.*

PSALM 98:4

Dear God,

    *Thank You for this day and all the days to come.
Even now, before our wedding day arrives, Father,
please begin to plan the joyous moments. Make spaces
for our laughter, carve out the unexpected moments of
joy and surprise, give us inspiration and creativity as
we search for ways to turn ceremony into celebration.*

Amen.

is God going to make me do something I don't want to do?

Search me, O God, and know my heart; try me and know my anxious thoughts. See if there is any offense in me, and lead me in the way everlasting.

PSALM 139:23–24

IF YOU HAVE INVITED GOD TO HELP YOU PLAN YOUR wedding, then it's quite possible that He is going to offer you some direction.

Obviously, He is not going to mail you a letter of suggestions for the reception or e-mail you a copy of His favorite vows. But if you ask Him to, He will definitely bring into your awareness things that need to be cleared up before you start a new life. And you may not like that.

In other words, God is going to ask you to be honest with yourself, and He's going to ask you to examine your reasons for getting married. Not that He wants to deny you the wedding you have dreamed of. In fact, I believe He wants to give you a wedding even greater than you first imagined! He knows that it takes more than a nice dress and a great cake to make a happy bride. The happiest brides I have ever seen had a sense of peace about them that came from knowing that as they started their new lives, there was nothing left undone in the old one.

And so God wants you to look into your heart and soul and be absolutely honest with yourself about all sorts of things. About the reason you are getting married, for example. If you are getting married for the wrong reasons, then God may ask you to stop planning your wedding and start evaluating your motives.

If you are having a big, lavish wedding, God may nudge you until you are clear about why. I don't think God wants to deny you a beautiful wedding, but He also wants to make sure that you aren't putting on a big show just to prove something to people who thought you were never going to amount to much or never find a husband.

God may whisper things to you that you don't want to think about at all. He may ask you to examine the wisdom of including anything flashy, pretentious, or insincere. You will recognize His voice if you have the nagging sense that your wedding is becoming a blowout party instead of an uplifting celebration.

I don't think God is a party pooper. But a wedding is a sacred thing, and it's as important to spend as much time on the content as you do on the form. Because the content of the wedding is not just the vows you speak or the words offered by the officiant. The content of your wedding is in the very spirit that you bring to the altar. And since God is a God of peace, I've found that He will keep whispering to you until you resolve anything that might interrupt that peace.

> *If it is possible, as much as depends on you, live peaceably*
> *with all men.*
>
> ROMANS 12:18

For me, my peace was threatened by an unresolved problem I had with an old friend of Jon's. She and I had had a terrible misunderstanding. The problem had been straightened out, and apologies had been given. But nevertheless things remained distant and awkward. I knew that Jon wanted her to attend the wedding, but he also didn't want me to feel uncomfortable. And I'll admit that I didn't want her there if I honestly couldn't be happy to see her. I went to the Lord and told Him my feelings. After praying about it, it seemed right go to the woman and make peace with her and invite her to the wedding. That is not something I wanted to do, but I trusted God and I did it.

As always, God was right. The woman and I reconciled sincerely, and Jon was pleased to have her at the wedding. More important, he was happy to see a burden lifted from both of us, one that could have come between us. As I watched her dancing at the reception, I smiled and realized that if I hadn't listened to God and if we hadn't worked things out, I would have deeply felt her absence that night and been saddened by it.

I know of many instances where an impending marriage has brought into focus a lot of unresolved issues with a bride and groom's friends, family, and with themselves. These are not things to ignore or overlook until the wedding is over. These are the very things you need to confront head-on if you want more peace and less drama on your wedding day. With all the other plans and responsibilities, dealing with more relationships at a time like this can seem overwhelming. But believe me, the time is now. And you'll be happier for it.

ideas to ponder

Therefore, if you are offering your gift at the altar and there remember that your brother has something against you, leave your gift there in front of the altar. First go and be reconciled to your brother; then come and offer your gift.

MATTHEW 5:23–24

THE IMAGE OF LEAVING THE ALTAR TO GET things right with others before you return is a powerful one. If you have unpleasant, unfinished business—particularly if you are in the wrong—your heart and your mind are divided between the holiness of the altar and the unholiness of the situation. That would be like walking into a sterile operating room without washing your hands; you don't want to contaminate the pure atmosphere at the altar, the place where something sacred is about to occur.

write it out

HERE ARE THE PEOPLE WITH WHOM I HAVE
unresolved issues. I don't know if I want them at my
wedding, but I know I don't want to carry the burden
of unforgiveness on that day.

_____

_____

_____

_____

_____

_____

_____

_____

_____

_____

_____

_____

_____

_____

_____

say it out loud

JUST AS I ASKED GOD TO HELP ME WITH the problem of my potential guest, you can ask Him about any aspect of your wedding that might be troubling you. Also, ask Him to reveal to you any areas that you haven't yet identified as problems.

Dear God,

There are people that I don't want to consider as we plan this wedding. I confess that I want to avoid them, ignore them, even punish them. I know that is not how You want me to handle this. But I have so many other things on my mind, I just don't want to deal with it. Please, Father, change my heart. Give me the courage and the desire to forgive and reconcile with those people. If I am using my wedding to impress others or to exclude others, if my reasons for getting married are not solid, or if there is anything else that You want me to come to terms with, I am trusting that You will show these things to me and give me the wisdom to handle them. Open my eyes and help me to do what is right.

Amen.

gathering the storm
all by yourself

GETTING MARRIED IS STRESSFUL ENOUGH. DON'T MAKE life tougher on yourself right now by assuming that there is a storm brewing out there over your wedding date waiting to rain on your parade. You are juggling your own expectations with your fiancé's and probably those of family members and friends. You have a thousand details to keep straight. For many women, this will be the biggest event they ever organize. As a result, brides have a tendency to obsess about everything that could go wrong.

Will the flower girl have a temper tantrum? Will the soloist come down with strep throat? By focusing on the potential for catastrophes, you are:

- taking time and energy away from positive acts of planning and of getting things done;
- forgetting to let go of the reins and hand them over to God.

On the other hand, negative prophecies do sometimes come true. That's because your instincts were absolutely on target, but you agonized in silence without doing anything about them. Maybe the flower girl, your three-year-old niece, is too young and too scared to be asked to rise to the occasion. Don't lose sleep over this. Talk to God. If you feel the need, talk to your sister or brother gently about your concern that you are asking too much of a small child. If your instincts are correct, the parents may well be as relieved as you are to get your niece off the hook.

Now, what about the soloist who might be coming down with something? Well, it's true. She might. You can hope she takes good care of herself, but there's nothing you can actually do to prevent her from losing her voice. If a solo doesn't get sung at your wedding, the wedding will go on. The lesson here is that after you make plans, make peace with the fact that the best-laid plans often go awry. Then stop worrying, because you've already put it all in God's hands.

There is a great danger in overplanning. If everything absolutely has to go just right, then maybe that's something you need to look at. Are you trying to prove that you can personally make everything perfect? Do you subconsciously think that your wedding will be a failure if it doesn't slavishly follow your script? Will your happiness that day depend on everything going right?

I remember that I specifically did not want a particular song played at our wedding, so I did not put it on the band's song list. However, someone requested it, and not only did the band play it, they pulled me and Jon up onto the floor to dance to it! I realized that the couple who had engineered this wanted to share "their song" with us as a gift and a blessing. It was a tiny bump, nothing to get excited about, but nevertheless a good reminder that you can't legislate your wedding if you're going to invite others to participate!

So do your best to get things organized the way you *hope* they'll go, then just relax. That way you'll be free to look forward to whatever your wedding day may bring instead of beating yourself up for not managing to orchestrate it all without a hitch.

Think of all the wedding stories you've heard told. It's always "what went wrong" that, in a funny way, is always the part people love to tell. My parents were married on a mountaintop in Nevada in 1940. It was a very simple affair with cookies and milk to be served after the ceremony. But the old-fashioned glass milk bottles had been placed in a nearby stream to chill. The bottles broke, the milk was lost, and forever after my mother's memory of her wedding was of milk flowing down the creek like a beautiful white ribbon. It's a remarkable, poetic image that has lasted a lot longer than any tears she may have shed over spilled milk!

ideas to ponder

HAVING REASONABLE EXPECTATIONS FOR YOUR wedding doesn't mean you shouldn't have any. Often brides scale down their expectations for reasons such as, "Wonderful things like that only happen to other people" or "I'm not perfect so I don't deserve all I want." But God wants "to do exceedingly abundantly above all you can think or imagine."

On the other hand, remind yourself that even the *one thing* that has to be perfect really doesn't have to be perfect. It may be getting someone special to attend the wedding or counting on a sunny day for an outdoor reception or even having your hair just the way you imagined it. Whatever you think *has* to happen just might not. And you'll be disappointed, but don't give it the power to steal your joy.

Body language is a powerful tool in prayer. Often I will catch myself clenching my hands fervently as I pray. But it's hard to feel like I'm actually letting go and "giving it to God" when my body is clearly trying to hold on! Next time, try keeping your hands relaxed and open. Sometimes I actually lay my hands out flat, palms up. It's amazing the difference it makes when you literally place yourself in a position of release, because you'll discover you have, at the same time, indicated you are ready to receive as well.

write it out

THE THINGS THAT I NEED TO STOP WORRYING about most are:

_____

_____

_____

_____

_____

_____

_____

_____

_____

_____

_____

_____

_____

_____

_____

_____

_____

_____

say it out loud

THIS SCRIPTURE WAS REPEATED MANY TIMES in the months before we were married. Try saying it out loud yourself:

> *We know that all things work together for good to those who love God, to those who are called according to His purpose.*
>
> ROMANS 8:28

Write this passage on a slip of paper and tuck it in your wallet. When storm clouds are gathering, take the passage out and read it.

As you say this prayer of release, try substituting *Father* for *God* and see if it helps you approach Him with a greater sense of childlike dependency and trust:

Father,
> *There are so many things I'm worrying about. Things I'm afraid will happen, things I'm afraid won't happen. Today, right now, I open my heart to trust them to You. Take away my worries, Father, and replace them with faith. Thank You.*
>
> *Amen.*

traditions or superstitions?

Something old, something new,
something borrowed, something blue,
A lucky sixpence in her shoe.

"Carry a lump of sugar in your glove, and your marriage will be sweet." "Carry a child over the threshold to guarantee fertility." "June is the luckiest month for a wedding." "If you cry on your wedding day, you'll have a long marriage." "Put an axe under your bed on your wedding night, and your first child will be a boy." "It's bad luck for the bride and groom to see each other on the day of the ceremony."

If you're getting married, then you will hear it all, the wedding superstitions, the cultural traditions, the bridal customs. I think it's safe to assume that you won't be putting an axe under your bed on your wedding night. (Of course, if I'm wrong, you might want to skip directly to the chapter on premarital counseling!) However, for the bride who wants to invite God to her wedding, superstitions and customs present a fascinating dilemma. If you believe in God and His power to transform your wedding and your marriage, then why put your faith in anything else?

On the other hand, there are numerous traditional bridal customs that are charming and sentimental that you probably want to observe. But it's important to make conscious decisions about the customs you choose and to understand their actual meaning versus the meaning you personally attach to them.

My friend Susan went to great trouble to present me with a very special gift a few weeks before my wedding. She had searched the rare-coin stores all over Los Angeles to find a real sixpence from the United Kingdom for me to wear in my shoe on my wedding day. The coin was even dated 1955, the year I was born. The idea, of course, was to fulfill the last line of the "something borrowed" tradition where the bride wears a sixpence in her wedding shoe for luck. Susan had done the same thing on her wedding day and later had the sixpence mounted in gold and placed on a bracelet that she often wore.

There are few things from our wedding day that we ever wear again. And so, having something as simple as a sixpence to point to and say, "I carried this on the day I was married," is a very lovely form of remembrance.

But, like most bridal traditions, the sixpence in the shoe originated not as a sentimental gesture, but as a very real superstition: wear a sixpence for *luck*. The list of such luck-related myths and old wives' tales is endless.

- It's good luck to carry a horseshoe to your wedding. (This was, not surprisingly, amended by the British to simply embroidering a small horseshoe into the hem of your dress.)

- It's unlucky to see pigs, dogs, or snakes on your way to your wedding. Doves, frogs, goats, lizards, and sheep are apparently okay. Ducks and chickens seem to be popular, too. But there are a lot of conflicting rules about cats. (Basically, keep the windows rolled up, and avoid zoos and farms.)
- It's bad luck for the bride to wear sharp or pointy things. (A bride who marries with knives hidden in her bouquet clearly has a rocky road ahead.)
- It was also good luck in England to be kissed on the way to your wedding by a chimney sweep. He represented the warmth of "the home fires" (and possibly a future of high dry-cleaning bills!).
- It's good luck to be married in the second half of the hour. That is, when the hands of the clock are on the upswing.
- If you marry on Sunday or Monday or Tuesday or when the moon is full or new, or if the month begins with the letter *J,* then good will certainly befall you. Or maybe it's ill.

Are you getting the picture? Wedding cake under your pillow, an even number of guests, a tossed bouquet, a caught garter—and I won't even mention the Limburger-cheese-on-your-wedding-night theory—all these good/bad luck superstitions actually get play at weddings. So many customs have been incorporated into the modern wedding that we rarely consider their ancient and sometimes disturbing origins.

For example, the bride stands to the left of the groom. This comes from the days when the groom actually stole the bride from the neighboring peasants and needed his right arm free to carry his sword in case it was necessary to kill any of her relatives.

"If anyone has reason why these two should not be married, let him speak now or forever hold his peace." The origin of this routine ceremony charge is a remnant from the days when women were actually chattel. Anyone who answered that question was more likely making a financial claim on his property than offering an opinion of the match.

Carrying a bride over the threshold was a Roman tactic to avoid an unpropitious stumble by the bride before she could be presented to the household gods.

Weddings, more than any other life ritual, seem to attract such traditions and superstitions. Women who would never carry a rabbit's foot or shake salt over their shoulder will actually wonder if rain on their wedding day is a bad omen.

It may sound petty to you, but at least give some honest thought to the traditions you embrace, especially if somewhere down deep inside you actually *do* attach some superstitious belief to them. This is important, because superstition began as a human attempt to control what could not be controlled or understood. But if you have put the future of your wedding into God's hands, "covering your bases" with superstition or other practices nullifies your belief that God can do what He has promised.

God plus a lucky penny, God plus a psychic, God plus a horoscope, God plus a numerologist—think about it. When did you ever hear of God needing anyone or anything else to accomplish His will?

Your future happiness is contingent upon the work you put into your relationship and the faith you put into God's ability to support it. You don't need a psychic or a horoscope, a lucky horseshoe or a fortuitous cat to ensure your plans for your wedding or your marriage.

For me, I chose to wear the sixpence in my shoe, not for luck but for Susan. I knew that it was her way of passing on love, not luck. And when she retrieved the sixpence and presented me with it later, hung on a gold bracelet, I was thrilled, and I will treasure it as a souvenir of my happy day and of her friendship.

I did the same with other traditions. I wore something blue, a small Fabergé cross that Jon had given me as a wedding gift. I wore something borrowed and old, an antique filigree pin sewn to my garter. My friend Leigh had spontaneously offered it to me at my wedding shower. I was touched at her gesture and honored to wear her grandmother's brooch. It brought us closer together when I wore it that day, and that was not luck; that was genuine sentiment. So was the ring that my dear friend Nina pressed into my hand just before the wedding as another something "borrowed." I wore it on my little finger. The whole "something borrowed, something blue" experience was fun and touching and made me feel like a bride. But it wasn't necessary, and that's important to remember.

There were other habitual wedding traditions that I chose not to honor at all. I have never enjoyed the rather demeaning sight of women diving for an airborne wedding bouquet. And my girlfriends don't need luck to find a husband; they need prayer and good references. Neither did I remove my garter to be tossed to a bunch of whistling and applauding men; there's something vaguely disturbing about seeing a bride sexualize herself to other men on her wedding day, and that's usually the tone of that particular ritual.

Much was made briefly about my choice of flowers. Someone gave me a book that explained floral symbolism in excruciating detail. Violets mean faithfulness, ivy is fidelity, daisies are loyalty. It soon became clear that virtually every flower that could possibly be found at a wedding signified something positive.

Surprise. I have yet to see a flower list in which petunias signify ten years of crankiness or lilies of the valley foreshadow financial ruin. Chances are any flower you pick will have something to do with purity, fertility, or love, although I seem to recall somebody had a real problem with yellow roses. Just choose the flowers you want. And if the symbolism of a particular flower appeals to you, fine. But remember, they're flowers, not magical investments in your future.

All this said, don't hesitate to enjoy the marvelous and rich traditions of symbolism. Cultural and religious symbolism at a wedding, as opposed to superstition, can actually enhance and deepen the wedding experience.

For example, at the end of most Jewish weddings, you will see the groom crush a glass under his foot. Historically, the act has always symbolized the destruction of the Temple of Jerusalem. Yet, through the years, the destruction of the glass has also come to symbolize the expectation that the couple will remain together until the glass is repaired (meaning forever). It can also represent a break with the past.

Some symbolic acts have grown out of practical necessity. Pre-Civil War slaves were generally forbidden to have a legal or religious marriage ceremony. And so a couple would often "jump the broom" as the only public acknowledgment of their commitment available to them. When African-American couples repeat this jump today, they are not simply affirming their love, but paying homage to their ancestors as well.

Symbolism, tradition, superstition. There *are* differences among the three. Most notably, symbolism in a wedding indicates hope; tradition honors our history and strengthens our connection to the past. Superstition, however, at its core, is rooted in fear. And there is no place for fear at a time like this.

ideas to ponder

A WONDERFUL AND HUMOROUS EXAMPLE OF the benefit of knowing your traditions comes from an American acquaintance of mine who was married to a woman in her hometown in Lithuania. At the reception, a three-day marathon, the bride and groom became the focus of a wild and rousing dance. Though he did not speak the language, he understood somehow that while surrounded by dancing wedding guests, he was supposed to hold his new wife in his arms as he stepped on a china plate, presumably to break it. Recalling the meaning of the broken glass in Jewish tradition, he stomped repeatedly and exultantly on the plate in an effort to crush it into as many irreparable pieces as possible. The horrified matrons of the town rushed to stop him, for the number of breaks in the plate repre-sented to the Lithuanians something very differ-ent: the number of children you will have!

write it out

THERE ARE POPULAR WEDDING TRADITIONS THAT deserve reconsideration, not necessarily to drop from your plans, but to be absolutely clear why you want to observe them. Write down some of the wedding traditions you have always assumed would be part of your wedding.

_____

_____

_____

_____

_____

Could any of the traditions you listed actually be considered superstition? Do you attach any real belief to any of them? Be honest with yourself.

_____

_____

_____

_____

_____

say it out loud

Dear God,

   Sometimes it is so tempting to rely on superstition or luck than to do the more difficult work of trusting You. Superstition is easier than faith in God because superstition asks nothing of us. You have asked much of me, and I must accept that You will also provide me with the means to accomplish the goals we have set together. Reveal to me, Lord, the worthy traditions and valuable symbols of marriage that have a valid place at our wedding. I commit to quiet my mind enough to hear Your voice.

Amen.

8

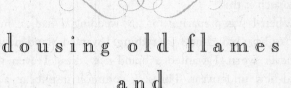

dousing old flames
and
severing soul ties

*Above all else, guard your heart with all
diligence, for it affects everything that you do.*

PROVERBS 4:23

THIS IS A DIFFICULT BUT IMPORTANT CHAPTER TO
write. As a Christian, especially as a Christian who has written
a television show about God, I have been in the unique position
of putting words in His mouth every week. I did my best to use
the popular angel characters from the show to represent God as
biblically and accurately as possible on a network television
series. It is an awesome responsibility, especially since I know
that every week I attempted to set forth ideal standards that I
value but haven't always lived up to myself. If, and whenever I
succeeded, it was surely by the grace and mercy of God.
Nevertheless, in my experience—especially in my failures—I
have found years' worth of stories to tell and lessons to share.

One of the greatest lessons I have ever learned never became an episode of *Touched By An Angel,* but it deserves a chapter in a book such as this.

When I was preparing for my wedding, I had an inherent need to have brand-new everything. I wanted brand-new shoes I'd never worn. I wanted a brand-new dress. I even wanted brand-new underwear. This is a common instinct as a bride. (Often, the only things that aren't new are your sentimental items: your grandmother's pearls, your best friend's bracelet, or your mother's veil.)

In the same way, there is often the desire to walk down the aisle with a new heart and a purified soul. Only here, you can't afford to hold onto anything old for sentimental reasons. You will have a need in your heart and your mind to come clean in every way that you can.

I will not argue the issue of premarital sex here. But I will raise some questions that you might never have considered before.

I grew up during a strange time in this country. When my sister Peggy was first married in 1961, I was a very small child, and the world still idealized the "typical" American family of the fifties: 2.4 children, two cars in the garage, and a television in every rumpus room. The American family, of course, was not actually typical at all. Underneath the perfect world of Westinghouse appliances and "Father knowing best" seethed a society of repressed emotions and repressed sexuality—even between married couples. That frustration finally exploded in the late sixties and produced a wild and inevitable swing in the opposite direction called free love and free sex.

I was just entering puberty then, and free sex sounded great because I associated it with freedom in general, and that's what every teenager wants no matter what decade they were born in.

I was long considered by my high-school friends to be "square." I went to church on Sundays, I didn't "go all the way," I called my parents and told them where I was on a regular basis. I thought I would be a virgin until my wedding night. But it didn't happen that way, and I didn't get married until I was forty-two. I never set up housekeeping with anyone. I lived alone for twenty years. I loved my independence and the latitude to go anywhere, do anything, and spend whatever I wanted without having to consult with anyone about it. But there were lonely times, too. And like many women I know, I was willing to trade all sorts of things, including my values, to ease that loneliness. Needless to say, I only ended up lonelier.

I don't think I fully realized the destructive power of some of my behavior until Jon and I seriously began to consider marriage. In a generation raised on the phrase "If it feels right, do it," I found plenty of support and justification for doing things that I knew weren't good for me. But sooner or later, they catch up with you, and when that happens, that is a terrible day. Nevertheless, through God's abundant grace, I realized that there was, in fact, a way to truly become new again and approach the wedding altar with the sense of a fresh beginning that I had imagined as a girl. The process began with the discovery of the existence of "soul ties."

RECOGNIZING SOUL TIES

> *No one sews a patch of unshrunk cloth on an old garment,*
> *for the patch will pull away from the garment, making the*
> *tear worse. Neither do men pour new wine into old wine-*
> *skins. If they do, the skins will burst, the wine will run out*
> *and the wineskins will be ruined. No, they pour new wine*
> *into new wineskins, and both are preserved.*
>
> MATTHEW 9:16–17

Soul ties are the strong emotional and spiritual attachments that you create with other people. These are not simply friendships or romances. They are something more, because in these relationships you have given away something of your soul and put it in the care or sometimes at the mercy of another person. Let's just say if you have a soul tie with someone else, I don't have to tell you what it means. You know.

You can't be a virgin again, but you can get rid of a lot of baggage before heading for the altar to meet the one man you had been looking for all along. And if you are a virgin, there may still be someone with whom you have a connection that could interfere with your ability to commit yourself body and soul to your husband. When you come into contact with an ex-boyfriend—a soul tie—and he says or does something familiar, it pulls the thread that still attaches the two of you. You get that old feeling. The pull is still there. That's why you have to sever the thread before you get married.

Someone once described it to me this way: When you get involved with someone—and certainly when you are intimate with someone—it's like gluing two pieces of wood together.

Then when you finally pull the wood apart, it doesn't come off clean. Each takes a little piece of the other away with it. The more relationships you have and the more sex you have, the more pieces of other people you are carrying around with you. And unfortunately, by the time you get married, the joy of sex and the thrill of discovery can be significantly diminished.

I am not making a moral judgment here. Sexual activity before marriage quite simply has the effect of bringing a lot of ghosts to the marriage bed. Period. That can result in guilt, jealousy, sexual dysfunction, and even a nagging sense of just not "being present" during lovemaking. I can remember talking to a number of girlfriends who, after they were married, remembered their wedding night with some remorse as "just another night like the ones that came before." Of more concern were women who expected the marriage ceremony itself to somehow magically erase their history.

BREAKING SOUL TIES

So how do you go about getting rid of all those glued-on pieces of other people? How do you get to the point where a man from your past has no pull anymore, even if he calls you by a term of endearment that no one else in the world knows about? Even if he looks into your eyes the way he used to when you thought he might be *the one*? Or even when, during a chance meeting, he says, "Why did we ever break up?"

The answer came for Jon and me during a retreat called the "Cleansing Stream." Along with many others, we were invited to write a list of all our past relationships, both sexual and emotional. I had names to put on my list and so did Jon. We approached this with complete honesty. As I wrote, I could feel how much I wanted back all the pieces of myself that I had left glued to other people. And how much I wanted to be rid of the pieces that were still glued to me.

When everyone in the room had completed their inventory, we supported each other in prayer as we brought each name on our lists before the Lord. We asked God to forgive us, and we committed ourselves to turn away from our past relationships and past behaviors. One by one, we crossed the names off. Finally, we ripped up our lists, threw the pieces on the floor, and acknowledged that the past no longer had any power over us.

Suddenly I felt healed and whole again, free of the pieces of other people that I had been carrying around. And all the pieces of myself that I had given away were gathered and returned to me. I hadn't felt like that in years. I felt cleansed and I was ready to marry Jon. I looked at him and smiled. He was now truly my one and only. And I was truly his.

ideas to ponder

I RESENT THE INSENSITIVE JOKES FROM PEOPLE WHO love to say, "Uh oh! The old ball and chain! Better hurry and have some fun before it's *all over!*"

Let's face it, you *are* getting hooked up to somebody. But there's a difference between being connected and being shackled, and it's important to understand that, especially to avoid any temptation that might present itself.

In the second book of Corinthians, Paul admonishes couples to "not be unequally yoked." This scripture is usually quoted when discussing interfaith marriage. But actually, it goes much deeper than that. A well-made yoke, fitting comfortably across two oxen, will allow them to walk side by side with neither one nor the other being rubbed raw by the wood that holds them together. Two oxen, well-matched, evenly tempered, and of the same size and strength can walk side by side, hauling quite a heavy load for a very long time, but if one decides to go in another direction, everything comes to a halt. Even the most comfortable yoke will chafe if you're always straining to look over your shoulder at what you've left behind.

write it out

ON A SHEET OF PAPER, WRITE THE NAMES OF people who have left pieces of themselves glued to you. Commit these names to God as you ask His forgiveness and His strength to help you turn away from old patterns in your life. Then cross the names off one by one, and ask Him to break the connections. This doesn't mean you can't see these people again. In fact, it means that you probably can see them again with a brand-new perspective and a healthy distance.

When you're finished, tear up the paper and throw it in the garbage. Write in the space below how you feel now.

_____

_____

_____

_____

_____

_____

_____

_____

say it out loud

READ ALOUD THE FOLLOWING QUOTATIONS from the Bible. Sharing this experience with your fiancé can be very powerful:

> *If any man be in Christ, he is a new creature: old things are passed away; behold all things are become new.*
>
> 2 CORINTHIANS 5:17

> *Forgetting those things that lie behind, I reach forward to all that lies ahead.*
>
> PHILIPPIANS 3:13

> *A righteous man falls seven times and gets up seven times.*
>
> PROVERBS 24:16

abstinence makes the heart grow fonder

To everything there is a season . . .
a time to embrace and a time to
refrain from embracing.
ECCLESIASTES 3:1,5

FOR NEARLY A YEAR BEFORE WE WERE MARRIED, JON and I decided to practice abstinence. We made the decision to become celibate as part of the healing work we did in preparation for our marriage. In twenty-first-century America the concept of celibacy is laughable to many people. "Who are you kidding?" is probably the most common reaction.

In fact, I remember the day I invited my mother to sing a solo at the wedding. My mother, from whom I have inherited my candid nature, announced unequivocally, "Alright. I shall sing 'Ave Maria.'" I shook my head. "But Mother, I'm not a Catholic." Mother arched her eyebrow and peered over her glasses. "What difference does *that* make? You're not a virgin, either!"

It's true, you can't go home again, and you can't be a virgin again, so why bother with abstinence? It's too late, it's too hard, and what purpose could it possibly serve to suddenly get an "attack of old-fashioned morality"?

Well, I don't believe God asked for abstinence simply to fulfill some moral code. Rather, like everything else He asks of us, there is a very practical purpose. If you think of the Ten Commandments, there isn't a single one that will actually make you happier if you break it. Coveting, adultery, murder, etc., aren't arbitrary taboos designed to control us; they are actions that cause pain to ourselves as well as to others.

As Jon and I prayed together each day, asking God to continue to show us how to prepare for our marriage, we began to sense that we should be apart from each other for a season so that God could work within us without the physical distractions that kept us listening more to each other than to Him. He wanted, as D. H. Lawrence wrote, for us to go "deeper than love."

> *Go deeper than love, for the soul has*
>   *greater depths,*
> *love is like the grass, but the heart is*
>   *deep wild rock*
> *molten, yet dense and permanent.*
>
> *Go down to your deep old heart, and lose*
>   *sight of yourself.*
> *And lose sight of me, the me whom you*
>   *turbulently loved.*
>
> *Let us lose sight of ourselves, and break*
>   *the mirrors.*

For the fierce curve of our lives is moving
again to the depths
out of sight, in the deep living heart.

In Chapter 8, "Dousing Old Flames and Severing Soul Ties," I told you about the theory that when you become intimate with someone, you are like two pieces of wood that are glued together. If marriage is a union, how can you be united by God spiritually if you and your fiancé have already united yourselves sexually? Abstinence in our case did not feel like punishment or limitation. It felt more like a prescription for recovery. We had asked God to help us, and He had given us an answer.

I remember sharing this "prescription" with a friend of mine who dropped her jaw and said, "Maybe you should get a second opinion!" But God's opinion was the only one that mattered to us.

We weren't exactly enthusiastic about the idea of abstinence, and it was hard to imagine the potential benefits during a time when we were trying to get closer. Nevertheless, Jon and I decided to "separate ourselves" in obedience to God.

Once the realization is accepted that even between the
closest people infinite distances exist, a marvelous living
side-by-side can grow up for them, if they succeed in loving
the expanse between them, which gives them the possibility
of always seeing each other as a whole and before an
immense sky.

RAINER MARIA RILKE
translated by Stephen Mitchell

During those months that followed, our conversations became more meaningful, more intimate, and more frequent. We took great pleasure in each other's company. The simple, quiet moments spent together reading aloud to each other or taking walks became more precious. Holding each other's hand and kissing were never again taken for granted. We discovered how to support each other with our commitment, complement each other's strengths, and to shore up each other's weaknesses. Knowing how the evening would not end taught us to savor our time together and to *listen*. So we learned things about each other that we had never known before. We also learned to trust one another completely, safe in the knowledge that if we could refrain from sexual relations, even when we felt great love and desire, we would be less likely to succumb to any temptation to stray outside the marriage.

Finally, our love for each other simply grew deeper. When the physical element was taken away, we experienced real spiritual and emotional growth. We realized that if illness or accident ever prevented us from having a sexual relationship, our marriage was not based on that alone and would survive. That is a tremendously empowering thing to know before you get married.

On our wedding day, after we had exchanged our vows and rings, but before Pastor Hayford pronounced us husband and wife, he asked us to kneel. He knelt, too, and prayed honestly and specifically. We had come a long way to get to that moment, and just because there was a roomful of people listening now, we didn't want to let the moment pass without acknowledging the miracle that had taken place. We had been "damaged property"; we had admitted it, and God had helped us to become new again. "Jon and Martha come to this wedding altar," Pastor Hayford prayed, "acknowledging readily their great need of healing grace in order to make the fullness of the future a very real hope. Seal this union by Your power and for Your glory. For we do believe, Lord, that this has not been a concoction of human mind or simply a surrender to mutual interest or human passion. We have sought Your counsel and You have directed us here, and so we come. . . ."

At the moment that Pastor Hayford said the words "human interest or passion," Jon's eyes filled with tears and he squeezed my hand. He got it. I got it, too.

After the benediction, we stood and Pastor Hayford pronounced us "man and wife." Jon took my hand, held it to his lips, and bowed to kiss it. Pastor Hayford smiled broadly and said, "More than that, Jon!" And Jon, my husband of just a few minutes, took me in his arms and kissed me.

The days and nights since have been like none that came before. We have never had sex again. We only make love.

ideas to ponder

You and I
Have so much love
That it
Burns like a fire,
In which we bake a lump of clay
Molded into a figure of you
And a figure of me.
Then we take both of them,
And break them into pieces,
And mix the pieces with water,
And mold again a figure of you
And a figure of me.
I am in your clay.
You are in my clay.
In life we share a single quilt,
In death we will share one bed.

KUAN TAO-SHENG
translated by Kenneth Rexroth
and Ling Chung

MANY COUPLES WILL RELUCTANTLY ADMIT they married mistaking good sex for real love. Only later did they realize they had no foundation for dealing with the other twenty-some hours of the day. A period of celibacy can teach you to solve disagreements by talking things out instead of using lovemaking as a way to avoid dealing with unpleasant issues.

write it out

IF YOU AND YOUR FIANCÉ AGREE ON A PERIOD of celibacy before the wedding, why not put it in writing? Make a contract with each other and God. Then if either of you ever finds that you want to change your mind, you can get out your contract and read it to remind yourselves why you made the choice to be celibate. This simple act can help you keep your promise.

say it out loud

HERE IS A PRAYER FOR YOU AND YOUR fiancé to say together at those times during your period of abstinence when you feel drawn to one another physically:

Dear God,

Thank You for the gift of physical love. We feel great desire to express that love now, but we feel an even greater need to remain apart during this time of spiritual preparation for our marriage. We want to come to the altar on our wedding day as two individuals so that You can truly unite us. Give us the strength to resist the pull of our passion until it is time for us to let it be a celebration of our commitment and the union You will have created.

Amen.

you don't want to, you don't have time, and you don't need it anyway

In every house of marriage, there's room for an interpreter.
STANLEY KUNITZ
"Route Six"

ENGAGED COUPLES DON'T USUALLY PUT PREMARITAL counseling on their list of things to do. It's often viewed as an inconvenience and even an intrusion on a busy time in your life. Others who consider it unnecessary will agree to it only because their pastor or rabbi will not perform the ceremony without some consultation. And yet, as much as most couples tend to resist it, I have never seen a married couple who regretted it. It's probably not a priority right now. But maybe it should be. Ask yourself: Are you spending more time planning your wedding than planning your marriage?

Jon and I, like a lot of couples, didn't think we needed premarital counseling. Also, we thought we were too busy to find the time for it. Anyway, we were in love. Wasn't that enough?

But even if your relationship feels like a match made in heaven, don't assume that it is just because you want it to be. Nevertheless, it's quite possible for a match that didn't begin in heaven to end up there. So you may want to go to God and be honest with Him about whether you have taken enough time to get to know the man you are planning to marry.

If the idea makes you uncomfortable, then that alone raises a flag. Are there issues that either or both of you are avoiding? Have you told yourself that you'll deal with the finances or the drinking or the communication problems after the wedding?

I invite you to read the following statements and to ask your fiancé to read them as well. These statements will certainly raise some questions and provide areas for you to focus on in counseling.

1. I can talk about my feelings with my fiancé, and my fiancé really listens.
2. I'm comfortable around my fiancé's parents and other family members.
3. I'm willing to spend time, including holidays, with my fiancé's family.
4. I'm comfortable with the way my fiancé handles money.
5. I will have no problem sharing my income with my husband/wife.
6. I feel included when I'm with my fiancé's friends.
7. I have problems with jealousy, even when my fiancé is simply spending time with friends.
8. Sometimes I need to be alone and my fiancé understands that.

9. I'm comfortable with my fiancé's habits and lifestyle. I can live with my fiancé's flaws and weaknesses even if they never change.

10. My fiancé and I can talk about our differences and resolve them without hurting each other.

11. My fiancé and I have discussed our expectations for sex in our marriage.

12. My fiancé and I agree on our plans to have or not have children.

13. My fiancé and I agree about how to divide up what needs to be done around the house.

14. My fiancé and I admire each other's successes, and we don't compete with each other.

15. My fiancé and I have talked about whether we would move if one of us got a job offer or a transfer.

16. My fiancé and I have some hobbies and interests in common.

17. My fiancé enjoys some hobbies and interests that I'm not involved in, but that's fine with me.

18. My fiancé and I enjoy each other's company, and we like to be alone together.

19. My fiancé and I think of our relationship as "the two of us against the world."

20. My fiancé and I have explored the cultural differences we bring to our relationship.

21. I feel completely committed to this relationship.

22. I support my fiancé in public even when we do not agree.

23. My fiancé and I share similar spiritual values.

24. My fiancé and I pray together.

I think couples often avoid marriage counseling because they are afraid that some third party will suddenly pronounce them "wrong for each other." But no one can decide for you whether or not you should be married; a counselor can only offer wisdom and experience to help you and your fiancé understand each other better and determine if you are entering into marriage with enough information about each other.

I know that Jon and I benefited immensely from the counseling sessions we had with our pastor and his wife as well as with a licensed psychologist. We counseled together, and, at times, separately. As much as you love and care about someone, it is still sometimes difficult to jump right into issues such as the ones listed above without the potential for misunderstanding. How many times have we said what we *didn't* mean on our way to trying to express what we *do* mean? In counseling I found not so much new information *about* Jon as a new way to explore issues *with* him. We learned to listen to what was said without necessarily attaching our own meanings to it.

We also enjoyed the opportunity to discuss our wedding plans with someone who was there to listen and help us sort things out rather than impose his or her own wedding expectations on us.

There is no prescribed length of time for effective premarital counseling, although some clergy will certainly request a minimum number of sessions before they will perform a ceremony. Ask your pastor or rabbi if he or she offers counseling or ask friends for a recommendation. One caveat: If you are currently in therapy, do not use your therapist. Find someone new to both of you who can offer a fresh and objective view.

I believe that the work we did together in therapy and counseling contributed significantly to our sense of peace and confidence on our wedding day. We had sought in advance a place where our romantic excitement had to take a break while we examined our long-term goals. And so when our pastor referred to love and commitment and our future, we knew that he understood exactly what that meant to us, and that added tremendously to the power of the wedding. We had all worked hard together to get to that moment.

Whenever I watch our wedding video, I always get a lump in my throat at a particular moment. Jon and I and our pastor have knelt in preparation to pray. As we listen to the choir sing, Jon looks up at Pastor Hayford. A knowing smile spreads across Jon's face and he nods. The minister almost laughs and nods back. Jon told me later that that was the moment when everything finally made sense—all the work, all the prayers, all the spiritual prep-aration, all the commitment that Pastor Hayford and his wife had asked from us—it all culminated in this amazing moment of grace. It's quite a sight to see two grown men with tears in their eyes share such an exchange.

So, please consider counseling. It will add a deeper sense of commitment to your vows in a way that you will only under-stand if you do it.

ideas to ponder

PREMARITAL COUNSELING IS NOTHING TO
be afraid of. Whatever you learn about yourselves
and about each other can make you stronger.

> *There is no fear in love; but perfect love casts*
> *out fear.*
>
> 1 JOHN 4:18

Every aspect of your life now as a single
woman—money, friends, sex, parenting, family,
friends, leisure time, religion, politics, and all the
rest—will also be an aspect of your life as a married woman. But remember, your fiancé is
bringing all those aspects into the marriage, too.
Most areas of your lives will overlap and blend,
but the ones that don't are the ones you want to
be prepared for.

write it out

AFTER YOU HAVE READ THE LIST OF 24 STATE-
ments on pages 99–100, list any concerns that have
surfaced and require prayer and counseling.

_____

_____

_____

_____

_____

_____

_____

_____

_____

_____

_____

_____

_____

_____

_____

_____

say it out loud

HERE IS A PRAYER THAT ASKS GOD TO help you prepare for premarital counseling:

Dear God,

    I make a commitment to leave no stone unturned in my preparation for marriage. Prepare my heart and my fiancé's heart to honestly and openly share any concerns that might exist about our wedding and our marriage. Help us find the time and grant us the desire to follow through on premarital counseling. Guide us to a wise adviser who will help us lay the foundation for a marriage that will bring us joy and peace, glorify You, and last the rest of our lives.

                                    Amen.

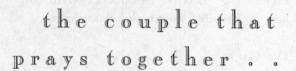

11

the couple that
prays together . . .

*Chains do not hold a marriage together. It is threads,
hundreds of tiny threads, which sew people together through
the years.*

SIMONE SIGNORET

THE FRENCH ACTRESS SIMONE SIGNORET MAY NOT
have been thinking about prayer when she talked of threads
holding people together, but daily prayer is without a doubt one
of the strongest threads in the fabric of your relationship with
your fiancé. And there is no better time than the present to
begin the habit, when the strains and stresses of wedding plans
can unravel even the strongest romance.

> *Cast your burdens upon the Lord, and
> He will sustain you.*
>
> PSALM 55:22

All you have to do is go to Him. While we were preparing
for our marriage, Jon and I began going to Him together every
day. This act was something I came to think of as our daily

"secret wedding." It was as though, in the privacy of our hearts and minds and the presence of God, we were letting Him know how firm our commitment was to marriage. We were also letting Him know how much we wanted to overcome obstacles and human foibles in order to make our union strong and lasting. And so we brought to Him our questions and concerns, both big and small. We talked to Him about our disagreements. We asked Him to help us know one another fully and love one another in spite of—or even because of—our human limitations and challenges. Then we thanked Him for His mercy, His love, and His guidance as we made our spiritual way toward the wedding altar.

> *It is a good thing to give thanks unto the Lord . . . to show forth thy loving kindness in the morning and thy faithfulness every night.*
>
> PSALM 92:1–2

Praying together every day changes you. For one thing, it is an incredibly intimate act between two people. Jon has never seemed stronger or more masculine to me than when he has humbled himself before his Creator to pray for our marriage.

Another advantage to praying every day is that it not only becomes a natural thing, but a necessary thing. You stop being self-conscious when you're talking with God. You stop worrying about taking up His time with your personal trials and tribulations. Establishing a daily routine of prayer is like having a hot breakfast every morning; there's a residual effect all day long, and it gets you through the day.

Daily prayer is also a little like the valve on a pressure cooker. (If you don't know what a pressure cooker is, don't worry.

You'll probably get one for a wedding gift.) Anyway, releasing the pressure on a daily basis in the form of prayer can be a wonderful protection against all your accumulated burdens exploding in one angry or destructive moment somewhere else. I've even found that some things will come out in prayer with Jon and God present that I realized I hadn't been sharing with Jon in regular conversation. Often our prayer time is followed by discussion about the deepest concerns that came up during our devotions.

There is a scripture in Proverbs 18 where God is referred to as our "High Tower," a place we can climb up to and see the world from His perspective. From there, worries and uncertainties, disagreements and arguments are viewed from a window of His love instead of from our own egos or vulnerabilities. High towers are also, by the way, safe places to be when you feel surrounded by overwhelming pressures.

I am always surprised to hear of couples who say they have never prayed together. Often they give the reason that it's embarrassing or too personal. Isn't it funny how people will do all sorts of private things together and never consider praying with each other? I suppose it's because we must ultimately be ourselves before God, truly naked with our fears and weaknesses utterly undisguised. Prayer makes you vulnerable. But God makes you safe.

ideas to ponder

WHEN WE TALK TO GOD, THE PRAYER ISN'T over when we stop talking. That's when the listening starts. He will always have an answer for you: "Yes," "No," "Not yet," or sometimes simply "Peace."

"What a Friend We Have in Jesus" is a beloved Christian hymn that has in its verse a message of wisdom for all of us:

> *Oh, what peace we often forfeit!*
> *Oh, what needless pain we bear*
> *All because we do not carry*
> *Everything to God in prayer!*

When we refuse to pray, we are saying that we would rather carry our own burdens no matter how heavy they are than trust God to be strong enough to take them away.

> *Prayer is the key of the morning and*
> *the bolt of the evening.*
> MOHANDAS GANDHI

write it out

C. S. LEWIS WROTE THAT PRAYER DOESN'T change God, it changes us. When we are honest with God, He is not surprised by what we tell Him. Rather, He is now able to help us because we have said that we are finally ready to accept His help. What are the burdens you have been holding on to rather than turning over to God? List them here.

_____

_____

_____

_____

_____

_____

_____

_____

_____

_____

_____

say it out loud

Be anxious for nothing, but in all things through prayer and supplication with thanksgiving let your requests be made known to God. And the peace of God, which surpasses all understanding, will guard your hearts and minds through Christ Jesus.

PHILIPPIANS 4:6–7

Father,

I confess that there are a lot of things I don't bring to You in prayer, either because I'm embarrassed or busy or because they're just too hard to say out loud. Teach me to pray, Lord. Help me to be bold when I pray alone and when I pray with others. Help me and my fiancé commit to a regular prayer time. Bless that time and use it to strengthen our relationship with You and with each other. Remove our timidity and teach us to boldly approach Your throne with our prayers and our praise.

Amen.

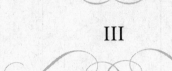

III

the engagement

AND

planning for
the big day

This marriage be wine with halvah, honey dissolving in milk.
This marriage be the leaves and fruit of a date tree.
This marriage be women laughing together for days on end.
This marriage, a sign for us to study.
This marriage, beauty.
This marriage, a moon in a light-blue sky.
This marriage, this silence fully mixed with spirit.

RUMI

translated by Coleman Barks with A. J. Arberry

12

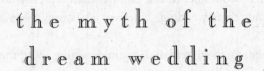

the myth of the
dream wedding

Ideals are like the stars. We never reach them, but like the
mariners on the sea, we chart our course by them.

CARL SCHURZ

THERE EXISTS IN THE MINDS OF MOST SINGLE WOMEN
the concept of the Dream Wedding. The dream is filed away
under SOMEDAY and gets pulled out and perused whenever some
promising man wanders into the romance zone. Some women
actually keep a real file of clippings and pictures of the perfect
wedding gown, the perfect cake, the perfect bridesmaid's dress. As
their tastes change, so do the clippings. And so do the men.

But generally, every woman will blush and admit that she has
been carrying a basic blueprint of her wedding in her heart for
years. When she finally gets engaged, the Dream Wedding suddenly becomes the Real Wedding, and the blueprint often
changes radically because of the one thing she hadn't factored
in: the groom.

If growing up is the process of creating ideas and dreams about
what life should be, then maturity is letting go again.

MARY BETH DANIELSON

Chances are your fiancé didn't play with a groom doll when he was a little boy. He probably never pored over the pages of *Bride's Magazine,* comparing china patterns or considering what his "colors" would be. In our culture, men typically don't fantasize about their wedding, whether it's twenty years away or next week.

Women, on the other hand, begin dreaming about their weddings from childhood. Even I, for whom marriage was never a priority, still found myself nurturing my own wedding fantasy over the years. It's hard not to when girls are bombarded from childhood by storybooks and fairy tales, toys and dolls, magazines and advertising that all send the same message: Brides and weddings mean growing up. While we're upstairs playing "getting married," all dressed up in Mommy's high heels and a lace-curtain veil, somewhere out there our future fiancé is playing "exterminate the monster with my subatomic cannibal blaster!"

So when the time comes to plan a wedding, it's no wonder that the bride is not only more prepared to take on the task, but in some ways she is unwilling to share it because she has already invested so many years of dreaming.

But let's think about this for a minute. If you're not including your fiancé in the wedding plans, are you setting a pattern of excluding him in the marriage?

It's quite possible that planning your wedding will be the first major project you and your fiancé have ever worked on together. For me and Jon, there was a great deal of excitement but not the same level of stress that many couples experience in the wedding-planning phase. For one thing, we had two dear friends who stepped in as wedding coordinators and who already knew our tastes and preferences. We had also just spent four years together completing a major project every week and putting it on television. In some ways, planning the wedding was a relief, because we didn't have to worry what the Nielsen ratings would be the next morning!

But usually, most couples have to tackle a lot of issues about teamwork and compromise for the first time when they organize a wedding.

I have found there are two sides to compromise. In one sense, it's a necessary component of marriage, and learning when and how to compromise might as well begin now. Why compromise? Because even though your fiancé may not be as imbued as you are with the how-to's of wedding planning, he might have some strong ideas about what he would like or what he definitely doesn't want. It could be that he doesn't even realize this until you ask him. Maybe he has in mind certain music, or a certain date for the wedding, or a certain place, or certain ways he would like his family to be included and honored. He could surprise you (and himself) with very specific answers. If that happens, you may be faced with the possibility of giving up something you've always wanted and substituting something he wants.

God willing, you're going to be married for fifty or sixty years. You're going to have to make a lot of joint decisions during that time—really big decisions like how to manage money, how to bring up children, where to live, what to do in a crisis. I remember thinking to myself, when Jon started to get really involved in planning the wedding, "Well, this is the man who could end up pulling the plug on me in a hospital someday. If I'm going to trust him with that, I'd better trust him to decide a few details of our wedding."

When Jon began participating more, he brought a sense of production and business to the enterprise that I could not have brought myself. As a result, we ended up with a much better wedding than I could have created on my own.

Notice, by the way, that I referred to Jon's *participation,* not his *help.* This is an important distinction, and one that's worth getting used to as you approach marriage. If your fiancé is helping you, then it's your job and he's just pitching in to lighten the load a little. If he's participating, then it's his job and his wedding just as much as it is yours.

But there is another side to compromise you should be aware of. Changes you make to your plans to accommodate your fiancé, or anyone else for that matter, should never make you uncomfortable. There is a difference between adjusting your dreams and completely surrendering your identity. There may be all sorts of reasons why your wedding may not match the original blueprint. But whatever your wedding finally becomes, be sure there is nothing included that you *don't* want. God wants this day to be one of harmony and happy memories and He knows that this is one of the rare times in your life when you can create a three-dimensional expression of what He has helped you and your fiancé to become.

You may have begun planning with your ideal wedding in mind, but your plans will inevitably culminate in a real wedding. However, you've invited God to help you, and He knows all about the Dream Wedding you've held on to all your life. Believe me, He knows how to make your Real Wedding better than anything you ever dreamed of.

ideas to ponder

Two are better than one because
they have a good return for their work.

ECCLESIASTES 4:9

YOU DON'T HAVE TO GO IT ALONE ANY-
more. You have an ally, an advocate, a partner—
someone to share not only the burdens but also
the blessings of life.

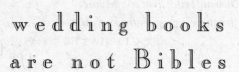

wedding books
are not Bibles

WHEN I GOT ENGAGED, I BOUGHT PRACTICALLY every wedding book that was ever published. I made the mistake of assuming that whoever wrote them must be far more qualified to plan my wedding than I was. I came to a different conclusion after I deliberated for days over the following books:

THE SIXTY-FIVE-DOLLAR, EIGHT-POUND COFFEE-TABLE PICTORIAL

This colossus has three hundred full-color pages of close-ups of napkin rings and centerpieces and personalized nut cups. The weddings are always held at someone's villa, and all the brides look like models.

This is the book you need to flip through to check out the wedding dresses and wedding cakes. You take this book to the caterer and point to the pages you've marked and say "something like this." This is a good book to help you visualize exactly what a one-hundred-thousand-dollar wedding looks like. This is not a good book to lie in bed and read at night. It will remind you of everything you've forgotten to include, hadn't even considered, and can't imagine paying for anyway.

THE ETIQUETTE BOOK

This is the book that reminds you not to post your invitation on the Internet, not to ask for donations to cover the reception, and not to include your gift registry in the invitation. The really exciting chapters deal with tasteful ways to combine your bridal shower with your sister's baby shower and the proper seating of your father and his new wife. This is a good book to have, because reading it will remind you that no matter how tough organizing this wedding seems, somebody else has it worse.

THE EVERYTHING-YOU-NEED-TO-KNOW CHECKLIST BOOK

This is the countdown book. It walks you through every crucial detail that must be completed six months before the wedding, three months before the wedding, etc. This is a good book to have, too. Except four months before the wedding, you'll be seven months behind!

THE MARRIAGE-VOW-AND-WEDDING-READINGS BOOK

Many couples begin their engagement with the best intentions of writing their own vows. They buy this book looking for ideas and usually realize that nothing anyone has ever said before can accurately express what they feel about their fiancé. It's a good book to find poetry and prose to include in the ceremony, but if you are going to write your own vows, don't start with somebody else's. Start with what's in your heart.

THE BOOK OF CUSTOMS AND SYMBOLISM

As I've discussed, there are good reasons to read up on the customs and traditions that you plan to include in your wedding.

Unfortunately, most of these books are more novelty than informational. It probably won't make any difference to you that wedding guests in Malaysia are given a hard-boiled egg to symbolize fertility. Your best bet is to read these books for amusement, not direction.

Don't let the glossy photographs and the endless lists intimidate or discourage you. Let them guide and inspire you, but don't feel pressured to follow every suggestion you read or live up to some unreachable standard. It would be a shame if you relied so much on the examples of other weddings that you felt your own was ultimately an imitation of something you saw in a book. Remember, God is the Creator. He said, "Let there be light." And there was. Imagine how He could inspire you to create elements of your wedding that are completely unique if you'll spend some time reading the Bible along with your wedding books and bridal magazines.

ideas to ponder

THE PHOTOGRAPHS IN WEDDING BOOKS and magazines are gorgeous because the stylists know all kinds of secrets that make the people and the clothes and the food look better than they do in real life.

The dress designer pins dresses to make them fit better. She stuffs tissue into sleeves so they puff out just so. The food stylist sprays fruit with water to make it look dewy and delicious.

And, of course, there are also make-up artists and hairstylists, and photographers with elaborate and expensive lighting tricks.

Finally, there's airbrushing, which erases crow's feet and blemishes and anything else that smacks of imperfection on the final print.

So while they may be inspiring, don't measure yourself or your wedding by the unrealistic standards you see in professional photographs.

say it out loud

Dear God,

I've looked at a lot of pictures of weddings and read a lot of words about what I should be doing to plan my own. Over the years, I've been to some beautiful ceremonies of my friends. Many of those friends will be at my wedding. Please show me how to stop making comparisons and just focus on pleasing You, my fiancé, and myself. Help me to let go of the myth of the Dream Wedding and create a wedding that is right for us.

Amen.

14

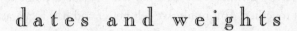

dates and weights

Love is a great beautifier.
LOUISA MAY ALCOTT

BE HONEST. HAVE YOU LOOKED AT THE CALENDAR and counted the days between now and the day you'll be married and calculated how much weight you can lose before then?

I have always struggled with my weight, but I always imagined that I would be at my thinnest and most beautiful on the day I got married. So have most women. I even know one woman who set her date according to how long it would take her to lose thirty pounds.

Think about this. Whether you are a size six yearning for a four or a size eighteen dreaming of a twelve, if you are marrying a man who knows you and loves you, it shouldn't matter. And believe me, dieting while planning a wedding will only add to your stress. It can shorten your temper and weaken your immune system and not only endanger your health, but steal a piece of your joy. The weeks and months before your wedding should be a time when you are having fun and enjoying the entire engagement and planning process. Let's face it, dieting isn't fun under any circumstances, and dieting with a deadline sets you up to fail. How would you feel if you walked down the aisle thinking, "I'm not what I wanted to be"?

For me, I resisted the temptation to diet and simply increased my activity a little every day. Jon and I made a point to take walks together. As a result, we felt better and had a guaranteed private time where we could discuss how things were going. We ultimately lost a few pounds, but it wasn't a goal we made for ourselves; it was a gift we gave to ourselves.

Now, I do think it's our responsibility to be healthy. And I know that I need to take care of this amazing body God has given me. However, since I've tried many times and many ways to get thinner over the years, I made peace with myself about this issue before my wedding. I knew that God would understand that I, being human, couldn't handle a weight-loss countdown at the same time I was working hard on spiritual issues. So I made a promise to God that after the wedding, I would seek His help to get physically healthy in the same way we sought His help to get spiritually healthy.

I bought myself a dress that fit well and that I felt comfortable wearing. I chose something that brought attention to my face, got my hair and make-up done professionally, and put on a great big smile. If you invite only the people who wish you the best and love you unconditionally, then that smile is what they're going to remember.

ideas to ponder

RUBY DEE'S FIFTY-YEAR MARRIAGE TO Ossie Davis provided us with not only one of America's greatest film and theatre couples, but also with a marvelous example of enduring love and commitment. When they appeared together on *Touched By An Angel* all of us on the set were struck by how utterly beautiful Ruby was and how terribly handsome Ossie was. And when they stood together, it was as though the lights of two individuals combined to create an even brighter flame. This is love that has taken years to perfect. This is real beauty.

The kind of beauty I want
most is the hard-to-get kind that comes
from within—strength, courage, dignity.
RUBY DEE

write it out

Do you have any goals to improve your appearance before your wedding? Write out those goals:

_____

_____

_____

_____

_____

_____

_____

_____

_____

_____

Now ask for God's help in achieving them and *let go* of your own time frame. *Let go* of the guilt for not having reached them yet. That guilt can be paralyzing and cause you to feel like a failure instead of a beautiful bride.

say it out loud

Dear God,

Please help me reach my goals to take better care of the wonderful body you've given me. Please, be strong, God, whenever I feel weak, and deliver me from condemning myself when I fall short of my own goals. Help me to be content and to stop looking for perfection in the numbers on the scale or my reflection in the mirror. Strengthen my confidence in the gifts and attributes You've blessed me with. I put these things in Your hands, and I trust that You'll show me, Lord, if there's anything I **do** *need to lose before the wedding.*

Amen.

15

the fifty-dollar
wedding

Where your treasure is, there will your heart be also.
MATTHEW 6:21

SPENDING A LOT OF MONEY ON YOUR WEDDING
isn't going to make you "more married." You could go down
to City Hall, pay fifty dollars for a license, and get married
tomorrow. I trust God would meet you there. True, you would
have foregone the joy of sharing a wedding with your friends
and family. But if you and your fiancé have agreed that you need
to save your money for something else (your education, a house, a
baby), then that decision makes sense.

Now, you're probably not going to opt for the fifty-dollar
wedding. But there are two essential lessons to be learned from
thinking about the possibility. The first is to realize that God
wants to be invited to your wedding no matter how modest it is.
We know He's not impressed by material wealth; He's interested
in spiritual wealth. So go ahead and spend whatever you can
honestly and comfortably afford, but there's no need to feel cheap
or embarrassed if you're working with a limited budget. Don't

let a florist or a baker or a wedding coordinator pressure you into forking over more than you should. And please don't go into debt. That's not an auspicious way to start your marriage.

More couples get divorced over finances than over any other issue. Even if the two of you have been sharing some expenses already, you won't truly pool your resources and make joint financial decisions until you're married. And that brings us to the second lesson. You've got to make this decision together. No matter who is paying for the wedding—you, your parents, or you and your fiancé—the two of you need to be the ones who make the budget and allocate the funds. In doing so, you will be establishing a working model for handling finances in your marriage.

Making a budget, whether for your wedding or for your married life, is all about identifying your priorities. It doesn't matter so much what your priorities are as much as whether or not you stick to them. For our wedding, a church and good music with a good sound system were particularly important to us. There wasn't a church on the property, as I've said before, so we allocated more funds to building a temporary one. And because we both love music so much, live music went up to the top of the list. Maybe music isn't such a big deal for you. Perhaps a fabulous location or a one-of-a-kind dress matters more. So adjust your budget accordingly.

These are not earth-shattering decisions. But you're practicing. You're learning about each other's values and spending styles. The budget is the least popular but perhaps most crucial detail of the wedding because it will have far-reaching consequences if not handled properly. Think of working out your budget not as a burden but as an exercise of how the two of you will be making financial decisions together the rest of your lives.

That way, it becomes a journey of discovery instead of an unpleasant chore.

Finally, don't forget to include God in this process. Don't assume He's not interested in money. Scripture tells us that He's interested in anything that affects your future.

ideas to ponder

THE WEDDING INDUSTRY IS EXACTLY THAT—
an industry that survives by making sales. Don't
let the siren call of an advertising pitch pull you
into making purchases that aren't in your budget. Ask yourself: "All my life, when I imagined
my wedding, did I really imagine handmade
parchment cones filled with silk rose petals
dipped in my signature perfume?" There is such
a thing as too much.

write it out

IMAGINE THAT YOU HAVE BEEN GIVEN A GIFT of $10,000 to spend any way you like, no strings attached. You can choose to put the money toward your wedding or you can use the money for something else. The point is to examine your priorities and learn something about yourself. Write down how you would allocate this sum:

_____

_____

_____

_____

_____

Now ask your fiancé if he would like to write down how he would spend the $10,000. Comparing and discussing your choices can teach you a lot about each other and get you started on the road to making prudent and pleasing mutual money decisions.

_____

_____

_____

_____

say it out loud

Dear God,

Help my fiancé and me to work as a team as we make financial decisions now about our wedding and later about our marriage. Give us the wisdom to value that which will nurture our spirits. Teach us not to associate a joyful wedding with a big price tag.

Amen.

choosing your bridesmaids

THE ORIGINAL REASON FOR HAVING BRIDESMAIDS and groomsmen was actually a practical one. In the days when keeping records was at best a catch-as-catch-can proposition, people needed witnesses to attest to the fact that a marriage occurred should there ever be any question.

These days, the selection of bridesmaids has become an honor to be conferred upon special friends whose presence with you at the altar is a way of telling them how much their friendship and support has meant through the years.

On the surface, this is a lovely idea. Until you remember your cousin who made you a bridesmaid at *her* wedding. Or you feel pressure because your fiancé's sister is feeling left out of your wedding.

Choosing your bridesmaids can become a stressful enterprise for several reasons. You don't want to hurt anyone's feelings, and you don't want to burden anyone with too much expense.

I have been a bridesmaid many times. And I have discovered a few great truths. First, most bridesmaids would have been just as happy to attend the wedding as a guest. Also, there is a level of stress for bridesmaids because it's probably the only time since they were six that someone is going to make them wear clothes they don't necessarily want to wear. Many appointed brides-maids would rather be left out than relegated to a line of ten or twelve. The whole idea of being a bridesmaid is that you're being acknowledged by the bride as someone special, hopefully not just someone to even out the wedding party.

Finally, I could have filled the aisles with all the women who mean something to me. I have sisters. I have nieces. I have friends from all over the country, some of whom had invited me to be a bridesmaid at their own weddings. Out of all these wonderful people, how could I decide who would stand up with me? How could I avoid hurting anyone's feelings?

If you are facing the same dilemma, perhaps my solution will help you. First, I decided not to worry about symmetry. If I had fewer bridesmaids or more bridesmaids than Jon had grooms-men, so be it. The Wedding Police were not going to ticket me.

Then I decided to pick one woman from each decade of my life. Each woman I chose had played a pivotal part at some important juncture in my personal development. I was forty-two, so I had four bridesmaids. Mary Ann is my oldest and best friend from elementary school. We climbed trees together, we were Girl Scouts together, we double-dated, stayed out late, and got in trouble together. We still share the special language and secret codes of childhood friends who can't imagine a life with-out each other in it. Gwen, the doctor I spoke of earlier, and my best friend from college, once picked up the phone and said, "Stop wasting time. You're almost *twenty-four* and you're getting *old*! Go to Hollywood and start writing!" Gwen has always had a way of making me get my act together, and we can still look at each other in silence and know what the other is thinking. Robin was my maid of honor, a woman whose faith and wisdom is matched only by her rapier wit. She is the best friend that everyone prays to find when you leave the nest and step out into the world and discover that it's full of awful things you never imagined, like property taxes and transmission problems. We have shared more tears and dreams than any other two women in California. If we don't talk every week, life isn't the same. And finally Marilyn, my dear, dear friend from my years in the television industry whose good sense, good taste, and tremendous patience have kept me going when talent, energy, and opportunity were at a premium. We have kept each other emotionally afloat in the treacherous waters of show business. So these were my four attendants, one from each important corner of my life.

When I explained my system, not one woman who wasn't included was upset.

However, the second part of my system was to make sure that even if people weren't included in the list of bridesmaids, they would be included in other ways. I wanted all of them to feel honored and cherished. Some of them read scriptures during the ceremony. Some of them sang. Others had special little assignments. Karen, for example, saw to it that my wedding dress made it from the wedding to the cleaners the next day.

I remember being a bridesmaid for a friend who, the last week before the wedding, suddenly discovered she simply had too much to do. She began to panic until some of her bridesmaids and friends jumped in to handle the little things like picking up the shoes and buying the panty hose. I felt more useful in the days before the wedding, just "being a friend," than I did on the wedding day being a bridesmaid.

If you can find meaningful ways to include your closest friends and relatives in your big day, you have, in a very real sense, chosen them all as your attendants.

ideas to ponder

I SPENT THE NIGHT BEFORE THE WEDDING in a small cottage on the property of the ranch where we were to be married. I invited a treasured friend, Karen, to "sleep over" and share my last night as a single woman. We had a pajama party, reminisced, played with make-up, looked at old pictures, and had a grand time. Karen helped me through the night just as my bridesmaids helped me through the next day.

write it out

MAKE A LIST OF ALL THE WOMEN WHO ARE special to you. Then look it over and find a common thread or theme that might guide you as you choose your bridesmaids from that list.

_____

_____

_____

_____

_____

_____

_____

_____

_____

_____

_____

_____

say it out loud

Dear God,

Thank You for the gift of friendship. Help me to express in words and deeds my appreciation and my love for each of the women who mean so much to me. Guide me as I choose those who will stand up with me, and guide me also as I seek ways to include more of my friends in the preparation for my wedding.

Amen.

dress for the best

Is not life more than food and the body more than cloth-
ing? . . . Why do you worry about clothing? Consider
the lilies of the field, how they grow; they neither toil nor
spin, and yet I say to you that even Solomon in all his
glory was not arrayed like one of these. Now if God so
clothes the grass of the field which today is here and
tomorrow is thrown into the oven, will He not much
more clothe you . . . ?

MATTHEW 6:25, 28–30

NOW, I DON'T KNOW ABOUT YOU, BUT I WENT OUT
and found a wedding dress as soon as I could. Before the date,
before the bridesmaids were chosen, before we picked out flowers or a location, I wanted that dress. For me and probably for
you, choosing your dress will make it all seem like it's really happening. You can try on a hundred dresses or the special one your
grandmother wore. But once you stand in the mirror and see a
bride looking back, you realize it's all true. You're really getting
married.

It's a great way to get the excitement going, but buying your
dress can also be a trying and exhausting proposition. So the
sooner you can get it out of the way, the more relaxed you'll be

and the easier it will be to imagine yourself as a bride while you make all the other wedding decisions.

What does buying a wedding dress have to do with God coming to your wedding? If He's invited, He'll be there no matter what you're wearing, but please consider something as you choose your gown. You are deciding what to wear at one of the most sacred moments of your life. You are going to the altar of God. It is not the prom, it is not a costume party. I have seen a number of brides who used a sacred occasion to play out their fantasies of being center stage. And it always began with the dress. Too short, too revealing, too suggestive. I saw a bride once whose dress was barely more than two pieces of cloth with laces holding them together. Nobody remembers the ceremony—we were all holding our breath waiting for the inevitable "snap!"

I'm not being a prude—there are great parties where dresses like that might make sense. But this isn't just a party. This is an appointment you've made with God and your fiancé to meet at the altar. Why would you wear something there that makes a bizarre fashion statement contradictory to the spiritual statement you are making that day? What are you saying if you kneel at the altar to pray and everyone sitting behind you is distracted by an overtly sexual or provocative outfit? Elegance and good taste will always be in fashion at a wedding.

ideas to ponder

ELEGANCE AND GOOD TASTE APPLY TO THE bridesmaids' dresses as well. My marvelously wise and creative friend Carol encouraged me and the rest of her bridesmaids to wear whatever made us feel comfortable to her wedding. Her only stipulation was that it had to be something colorful. Since I, like so many women, have a closetful of bridesmaid's dresses that aren't particularly flattering, I wore a favorite red silk cocktail dress. It was a relief to know that I was wearing something that was just right for my body and that I wasn't in danger of being compared to three or four other women wearing the same dress.

write it out

THE WEDDING DRESS I WILL FEEL MOST COM-
fortable being married in will have the following
characteristics:

_____

_____

_____

_____

_____

_____

_____

_____

_____

_____

_____

_____

_____

_____

_____

say it out loud

Dear God,

   All my life I've looked at wedding dresses, and I've wondered when the day would come when I'd have the chance to choose my own. Now the day is finally here, and I want this dress to be perfect. Lord, help me to recognize it when I see it. I know it's just a dress, but I also know that You understand the desires of my heart.

                                        Amen.

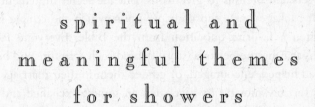

spiritual and meaningful themes for showers

THE SHOWERS YOU'LL NEVER FORGET WILL NOT BE the ones where you got a lot of gifts but the ones where something personal and emotional took place. I'm going to share with you three ideas that made memorable showers—two that were given for me and one that I gave for a friend.

THE SCRIPTURE SHOWER

There is a married couple I've known for fifteen years who are the essence of blissful marital happiness. They finish each other's sentences, they call each other "pal," and they have finally started to look like each other. They have the incredible gift of still being able to amuse and fascinate each other after nearly two decades of marriage, two children, and many ups and downs in their careers. They surely must have disagreements, but they are obviously soul mates. And they are the ones who knew instinctively that, more than material gifts, Jon and I needed wisdom and good advice from friends who "have been there."

This creative couple hosted a shower for us where all the guests were married couples. At first, it did seem like a typical shower because the guests had bought and wrapped kitchen gadgets and utensils to give to us. But the secret ingredient in each package was a slip of paper upon which the couple had written a favorite quotation from the Bible. Everyone took turns sharing the personal story behind each scripture and how it had helped, encouraged, or guided them in their marriage. It was terribly moving to have such an honest exchange and to receive gifts that would truly last a lifetime.

As a result of that evening, Jon and I started our marriage with a personal collection of verses from God's Word from people who had succeeded in their own marriages. Not only were they mounted in a beautiful book for us, but many of the scriptures from the shower became part of our wedding ceremony. One is inscribed on the inside of Jon's wedding ring: "We love because He first loved us" (1 John 4:19).

WINE-AND-BOOK SHOWER

On this occasion, the hostess asked each guest to bring a well-loved book and a bottle of wine. Some books were new, some rare and used, some came straight from a friend's own bookshelf. As I unwrapped each book, the friend who gave it presented an informal "book report" to the rest of us, explaining why it meant so much to her and why she wanted me to have it. There was a first edition of a work by Edna St. Vincent Millay. Another was an out-of-print book one friend decided to part with so I could have it. There was a beloved children's book, a brand-new best-seller, a tiny book of prayers. I now have a library of special books that I will cherish forever, each with a tender inscription from a dear friend.

As for the wine, we shared some of it while toasts were made during that festive get-together. The rest of the vintages went home with me to age and be opened on anniversaries to come, when Jon and I would make some toasts of our own.

SCRAPBOOK SHOWER

I gave this shower for my friend Robin and her husband, John. I got the idea from the recently popular custom of asking party guests to bring a note or card to be included in a scrapbook. It occurred to me that it would be a lot more fun and more meaningful to have the creative stuff go on during the shower rather than before. I bought a big scrapbook, plus all sorts of decorative potpourri such as stickers and ribbon, glue, glitter, felt-tip markers, magazines to cut up, etc. I also had cameras, film, and a printer. Everyone at the party just sat around and talked about memories and wrote them down. We snapped pictures of each other, and people got creative in making their pages look special. It was a warm and happy evening for all of us, and a marvelous icebreaker as people got to know each other while sharing the scissors! And now Robin and John have a one-of-a-kind memento.

ideas to ponder

WHEN FRIENDS OFFER TO GIVE YOU A SHOWER, you may want to suggest that they share the responsibility with other friends who are also hoping to host showers for you. This can help financially as well. My friends did this, and as a result, I had three large, very different showers. They were divided into three categories: friends from work, old friends, and new friends. It worked beautifully. Each one had a very unique tone, and no one felt obligated to attend more than one.

I kept the ribbons from my showers and made them into a bouquet. I carried it, with all its memories of my beloved friends and their best wishes, down the aisle at the dress rehearsal. It has survived much better than my actual wedding-day bouquet, and I still treasure it.

Whenever I have hosted a shower, I have always asked the guests to go around in a circle, introduce themselves, and tell the rest of the group how they know the bride. It has invariably become a deeply emotional part of the shower. At my own, I recall great laughter and many happy tears as my girlfriends reminded me of all we had shared over the years.

If you don't have a Scripture Shower, you may still want to create a book of marriage-related scriptures to include in your ceremony or simply to consult over the years. Here are a few from our own book:

> *Trust in the Lord with all your heart and lean not on your own understanding; in all your ways acknowledge him, and He will make your paths straight.*
>
> PROVERBS 3:5,6

> *Two are better than one, because they have a good return for their work: If one falls down, his friend can help him up. But pity the man who falls and has no one to help him up. Also, if two lie down together, they will keep warm. But how can one keep warm alone? Though one may be overpowered, two can defend themselves. A cord of three strands is not quickly broken.*
>
> ECCLESIASTES 4:9–12

> *Therefore, as God's chosen people, holy and dearly loved, clothe yourselves with compassion, kindness, humility, gentleness, and patience. Bear with each other and forgive whatever grievances you may have against one another. Forgive as the Lord forgave you. And over all these virtues put on love, which binds them all together in perfect unity.*
>
> COLOSSIANS 3:12–14

We love because He first loved us.

1 JOHN 4:19

And now, brothers, as I close this letter, let me say this one more thing: Fix your thoughts on what is true and good and right. Think about things that are pure and lovely, and dwell on the fine, good things in others. Think about all you can praise God for and be glad about.

PHILIPPIANS 4:8

. . . Don't urge me to leave you or turn back from you. Where you go I will go, and where you stay I will stay. Your people will be my people and your God my God. Where you die I will die, and there I will be buried. May the Lord deal with me, be it ever so severely, if anything but death separates you and me.

RUTH 1:16,17

May God who gives patience, steadiness, and encouragement help you to live in complete harmony with each other—each with the attitude of Christ toward the other. And then all of us can praise the Lord together with one voice, giving glory to God, the Father of our Lord Jesus Christ.

ROMANS 15:5,6

If you fully obey the Lord your God and care-fully follow all His commands I give you today, the Lord your God will set you high above all the nations on earth. All these blessings will come upon you and accompany you if you obey the Lord your God: You will be blessed in the city and blessed in the country.

The fruit of your womb will be blessed, and the crops of your land and the young of your livestock, the calves of your herds and the lambs of your flocks. Your basket and your kneading trough will be blessed.

You will be blessed when you come in and blessed when you go out.

The Lord will grant that the enemies who rise up against you will be defeated before you. They will come at you from one direction but flee from you in seven. The Lord will send a blessing on your barns and on everything you put your hand to. The Lord your God will bless you in the land He is giving you.

The Lord will establish you as His holy people, as He promised you on oath, if you keep the commands of the Lord your God and walk in His ways.

DEUTERONOMY 28:1–9

And the Lord shall guide you continually and satisfy you in drought and dry places and make strong your bones. And you shall be like a watered garden and like a spring of water, whose waters fail not.

ISAIAH 58:11

I thank God for every remembrance of you.

PHILIPPIANS 1:3

The Lord bless you and keep you; the Lord make His face shine upon you and be gracious to you; the Lord turn His face toward you and give you peace.

NUMBERS 6:24–26

write it out

PREPARING YOURSELF FOR YOUR WEDDING AND your marriage is not just about the future, but about making sure you don't lose the friendships you've developed in the past. Showers are one way of connecting with the important people in your life. They can be occasions when you remember good times as well as the troubled moments when you were there for each other. But in this mobile society, not all of your friends can gather in a room to spend an evening with you. Why not reach out to all those who are close in spirit but far away in miles? Send an e-mail, send a fax, or send a letter. You can even have a shower "on-line" or a conference-call shower. Remember, it's not about unwrapping gifts, it's about reaffirming friendships. It's an important rite of passage on your way to your wedding. Make a list of people who may not be able to attend a shower but with whom you want to connect before the wedding.

_____

_____

_____

_____

_____

_____

say it out loud

Dear God,

Thank You so much for my friends, for the memories we have made, for the tears we have shared, and for their support as I prepare to marry.

Bless the times we will share in the coming weeks. Remind us that every good friendship is a miracle and that miracles come from You. Thank You.

Amen.

19

the courage to make
the guest list

THERE IS PERHAPS NO OTHER OCCASION THAT OCCURS
in life when you are called upon to make a list of everyone you
know and care about and then essentially rank them in importance. It is a harsh truth to realize that this is what you're finally
doing when you create your guest list.

Additionally, with each name on your list comes a memory and a personal connection. It is literally exhausting to go
through name after name after name not only because it is time
consuming, but because it's emotionally draining. This is an
inventory of practically every important relationship in your
life. You must not only weigh why you're inviting some people,
you must also consider why you are not inviting others.

When we first discussed a wedding, Jon mentioned how very
much he wanted to get married very simply and quietly under a
tree with twelve people. I was perfectly happy with that. Until I
tried to pick my six people. It didn't take us long to realize that
between our combined family and decades of friends, there
were too many people we would miss. It may be helpful to note
the criteria we used: "Who would we miss?" Not, "Who wants
to be there?"

157

We ended up with 155 friends and family, and we still had to exclude people with whom we had warm relationships. Nevertheless, I am proud of the choices we made and how we made them. We learned some lessons along the way that I want to share:

First of all, we did not invite anyone out of obligation. The business friends who attended, for example, were there because we liked them, not because we were returning a social favor or using our wedding to solidify a business connection.

Second, we prayed for guidance in creating the guest list. Remember that His presence at our wedding was a blessing to everyone there. So who knew better than God who should be there to receive it?

Third, it became very clear that the people who would attend our wedding had to be there for one purpose: to genuinely share our joy. There should never be anyone at a wedding who cannot be happy for you that day. There will inevitably be a few friends who bring dates and escorts that you don't know, and of course you will want to make them feel welcome. But it is very important to avoid what I call The Toxic Guest.

THE TOXIC GUEST

Just as you have invited God to bring extra blessing to your wedding, you may want to think twice before inviting anyone you can reasonably predict will bring only "negative vibes." That holds true even if the potential toxic guest is your uncle or your godmother or your mother's best friend or your father's business associate. This is your day, and even though you want to be a good hostess, this is not the day for you to bear the burden of family problems or old enmities or people with bad attitudes who should know better. You deserve to make the choice not to include those who will poison the occasion by getting drunk, by getting angry, or by sitting in the corner criticizing the wedding or speculating on how long the marriage will last. These things are unacceptable and chances are you already know who that potential perpetrator is.

It doesn't matter who is paying for the wedding. You have a right to prevent anyone from attending who will make you, your fiancé, or your guests uncomfortable.

This is why it takes courage to make the guest list, because we all have a tendency to avoid discussing touchy situations and difficult people if we don't have to, especially within our own families. But weddings always force these issues to the surface. So be strong and be honest and also be kind. It is important that you do this together. Ask God to help you speak the truth with love. Sometimes it even takes something like a wedding to bring about change and awareness in people. Don't underestimate God's power to use a seemingly unresolvable problem to affect healing.

THE PAST SHOULDN'T BE PRESENT

Generally speaking, ex-boyfriends don't belong at your wedding. Your relationship may have ended long ago and the two of you are on friendly terms now, but what are you saying to your fiancé when you ask him to welcome someone to his wedding who has shared intimate moments with his bride? The message you are sending is that you're still in some way emotionally involved with this man. And even if you manage to justify it to your fiancé, why put him through it? How would you feel if he invited an old girlfriend? If it's that important to you to have a former love there, then ask yourself if you have truly done the spiritual work you needed to do in preparation for this wedding.

If you haven't gotten rid of what we've identified earlier as the soul tie, the glued-on pieces of a previous intimate relationship, please flip back to Chapter 8, and ask God to help you shed those ties. Then consider crossing your past relationships off your guest list.

Inevitably you will still have to deal with other guest-list challenges such as ex-wives, stepchildren, estranged relatives, etc. However, with God as an ally you have a new way of dealing with problems. When your patience runs out, draw on His. When your human understanding is stretched to the limit, ask Him for the divine kind that never fails. When you look at a name on a list and see only trouble ahead, turn that person over to God in prayer. Remember, the spiritual element in your wedding will be a result of the grace of God and the spiritual preparation you have done. And how you treat others at this time is a reflection of that as well.

ideas to ponder

THIS MAY BE "YOUR DAY," BUT BEING A bride does not make you royalty. You are not summoning people to your court to perform, so consider the differences between being a hostess and a princess. Try not to invite more people than you can realistically spend a few meaningful moments with. I attended a wedding once where I was one of six hundred guests. The bride was simply a distant white blur across the ballroom. One disgruntled guest, a film director, mumbled: "Now I know how it feels to be an extra."

There will inevitably be people and things you can't control on the day of your wedding. A serene and peaceful acceptance coupled with a quiet prayer of release will ultimately result in a happier day.

write it out

A GOOD EXERCISE WHEN DRAWING UP A FIRST
draft of your guest list is to give yourself three minutes to write the names of everyone you would like
to be at your wedding. If at any time during those
three minutes you have to stop and think of more,
then put down your pen and look at the names you
already have. That should be a good indication of the
people you know you can't do without. Make your
"three-minute" list here.

_____

_____

_____

_____

_____

_____

_____

_____

_____

_____

_____

say it out loud

Dear God,

   I know that I make mistakes and that it is not my place to judge other people. But, Lord, there are those among my family and friends whose actions have the potential to ruin the holiest, happiest day of my life. Grant me the wisdom to identify these people and to deal with them lovingly and yet decisively.

   I turn each one over to You.

Amen.

saying good-bye to the single life

Strength and dignity are her clothing and she can smile at her future.

PROVERBS 31:25

DON'T BE SURPRISED IF YOU EXPERIENCE SOME FORM of the infamous pre-wedding jitters. In the midst of all the planning, something might trigger a sense of panic. You're getting married. This is a huge step, a life-changing event of such magnitude that you'd have to be superhuman not to feel a little anxiety about the future and a certain wistfulness about the past. But in fact, you are very human, and your pre-wedding jitters are not just a natural part of getting married, they can be constructive as well. Research has shown that the human body can't distinguish between a negative stimulus and a positive one, so even though you're happy and excited about your upcoming wedding, you're bound to experience stress. But sometimes the stress you feel may actually be serving a good purpose.

I didn't feel any jitters at all until my bridal serenity finally cracked on the morning of my wedding. Robin and Gwen were hosting a bridesmaid's luncheon at a nearby Italian restaurant. They had chosen it because it was cozy and charming with a fireplace and pretty gardens. I had wanted to spend my last hours as a single woman with not only my bridesmaids but also my sisters and nieces and closest girlfriends. I had imagined the time would be not so much to honor me as to honor all the years of sisterhood and loyalty that would be represented in that room.

Two days earlier, I had shipped twenty gift-wrapped boxes of Waterford crystal champagne glasses to the restaurant with the instructions to hold them for "the Williamson Wedding Party." When I arrived Saturday morning, I expected to see one box at each place setting as surprise gifts for my friends.

But the boxes were not there. I asked the maitre d', "Where are the twenty white boxes?" He smiled, and said, "The ones for the wedding party?" I nodded. "Don't worry," he said. "I gave them to the wedding party last night."

It took a full minute before the reality set in. He had given away every one of the boxes to other people celebrating another wedding. They were terribly grateful and impressed with the restaurant's remarkable generosity. They had taken my gifts and gone home.

I don't think it was the actual cost of all that Irish crystal that made me begin to sob. I just didn't want the day to go by without giving a special gift to my friends.

Girlfriends—real friends—are great. They will be the first to tell you that crying four hours before your wedding will make your eyes puffy. They will be the first to tell you that they don't need crystal champagne glasses anyway and that the greatest gift of all is just being here to share the day. They will also tell you to go ahead and cry now and get all the tension out. And so I did. I just cried and cried and cried. I "cried for happy" as my mother puts it. I had all the women in my life in one place, and I didn't have to explain a thing. They all understood.

That was definitely a good glitch on my wedding day. The brunch might have happened with all the crystal in attendance, but I know that I never would have had such a good, cleansing cry. I needed that. I needed somehow to deeply and honestly and emotionally say good-bye to being single. And there was no better time for it than with all the friends who had dried so many lonely tears in the past.

When we agree to marry someone, the reality of what we are about to do has a way of presenting itself to us by degrees. Often we don't even realize the level of stress that we are operating under, and if you don't acknowledge it, it can undermine your sense of peace. You may need to allow yourself to cry and experience the very real emotions of loss and grief that go with saying good-bye to your old way of life. It is healthy, it is necessary, and you don't have to explain it to anybody. Just find a safe place to express it. Ask God to grant you the wisdom to deal with your nerves in healthy ways. Prayer, meditation, and a soothing herbal bath are a lot better than one drink too many or a midnight raid on the refrigerator, neither of which ever solved anything.

ideas to ponder

Resist the temptation to say farewell to singlehood with a raucous night of drinking and male strippers. After all the spiritual work you've done, it feels like a backward step. If a runner is getting ready for a race, she tries not to "break training," because she doesn't want to jeopardize the race or risk injury. Don't underestimate the diminishing effect of celebrating your upcoming marriage with "last flings" or reckless "beefcake" parties, which emphasize that your wedding is an ending rather than a beginning.

One constructive and very fun "bachelorette party" can be a night of watching old romantic videos together or looking through photo albums and remembering fun times with your girlfriends. My Colorado friends take pre-wedding hikes or bike rides. Perhaps you can plan something to do together in the future after you're married. Remember, girlfriends may experience a little stress, too, as they wonder how they will fit into your life once you are married.

write it out

Write out the things that you think you will miss about being single.

_____

_____

_____

_____

_____

_____

Now, write out the things you are looking forward to in marriage that you never had as a single woman.

_____

_____

_____

_____

_____

_____

_____

say it out loud

Dear God,

Sometimes when I think about being married, I wonder if I'll miss the sense of independence that I have now, and I don't want to lose my identity as an individual. It's funny to feel nostalgic about the single life when I know that what I really want is to be married to the man I love. But I wonder sometimes if I can really make all the adjustments that living my life with another person will require. I am trusting You to help me, and I am not going to worry about it now. I put my future in Your hands and I thank You that You brought such a wonderful man into my life.

Amen.

the only two things that will finally matter

IT'S THE NIGHT BEFORE YOUR WEDDING. AFTER ALL the planning and all the details, all the worrying about the flowers and the agonizing over the cake, only two things are finally going to really matter tomorrow. Did you marry the right man? Did you wear the right shoes? Because if either of these don't fit, you'll be miserable.

If you've done the spiritual planning and the praying, then you already know if you have the right man.

As for the shoes, break them in. Do not under any circumstances wait until your wedding day to wear them. Wear your wedding shoes for two or three hours a day for a few weeks before the wedding. If they still aren't comfortable, find another pair. Trust me. There is nothing like aching feet or a painful blister to ruin even the happiest of days.

Once you've got the man and the shoes that fit, once the invitations are out and the details are finalized, there is nothing left to do but trust God.

Don't be tempted now to obsess over the details on your checklist. The plans have been made, the assignments have been given. A good idea is to ask someone you trust to be on "Last-Minute Details Duty." Inevitably, you'll think of something you've forgotten. Don't try to take it all on yourself now. Turn it over to that friend, and let her take it off your hands and off your mind.

Be prepared for any potential problems that you can foresee, but realize that other problems might arise that you could never be prepared for. Decide in advance to put those things in God's hands.

Anticipating what can go wrong is part of my job as a producer. So I tried to back myself up with all sorts of contingency plans in case of a wedding disaster. I had the phone numbers of emergency doctors, dentists, even manicurists written down on a card. I had extra panty hose, extra shoes, extra contact lenses. The only thing I didn't try to double was my fiancé! Even with all that preparation, I could never have anticipated the one thing that actually went really wrong.

That Friday night before the Saturday wedding, family and relatives arrived at the San Ysidro Ranch and checked into their cottages, which were scattered across several acres in the beautiful hills above Santa Barbara, California. We gathered before dinner for the dress rehearsal in the "tent church" we had erected. Moments into the rehearsal, we were interrupted by the earsplitting sound of sirens and helicopters.

It appeared that a man in a stolen truck was being pursued by the police. He had tried to escape by following a road that unfortunately dead-ended right at our wedding site. The man hit the brakes and jumped out of the truck. The police drew their guns and ordered him to "Freeze!" But the man refused and ran into the woods that surrounded the ranch. For the rest of the night and most of the following day, there was a fugitive loose on the property. More helicopters came; police dogs tracked the man; and there were rumors that he'd had a scuffle with one police officer and had taken his gun. Needless to say, it lent a certain drama to the pre-wedding festivities. No one could walk back to their rooms without an escort, and all windows and doors had to be locked in this normally secure and peaceful resort.

A few years ago my first instinct might have been to despair and pronounce my wedding officially ruined. But now I reacted very differently. This first crack in our "perfect wedding" was the moment when we realized that God had, in fact, shown up for the wedding as promised and was now asking us to put into practice all that we had been rehearsing for months. And so, despite the chance that an armed fugitive could walk in at any moment and take us all hostage, we all gathered together and prayed for him. That man was going through what was probably the worst day of his life just as we were about to experience the best day of ours. The incident had a galvanizing effect on the entire wedding party, and we were all given a great lesson in perspective. Heavy rains were predicted and might prevent some guests from attending; there was even concern about getting enough electricity to the tents. But no disappointment that could befall us in the next twenty-four hours was going to match the miserable night and the day ahead for this poor soul. I couldn't help but think that even though I certainly would have preferred that the fugitive thief had taken another road that night, had he ended up somewhere else instead of with us, he would not have had so many people praying for him.

Prayer is a very important element of the night before your wedding. Be sure to find time to pray with your fiancé. Pray for the day, not to be perfect, but to go according to God's plan. Pray for the safety of guests who are traveling to the wedding. Pray for wisdom and inspiration for your minister and for others who are participating in the ceremony. Pray for those with heavy responsibility and those assigned particular tasks. Pray for a spirit of joy and love to prevail throughout the event. And don't forget to thank God for all He has done to bring you to this moment.

Jon and I had decided not to see each other the next day until the ceremony, not for good luck, but because we just liked the idea that the next time we would see each other would be at the altar. And so, with police dogs barking outside, helicopters whirring above, and police radios squawking, we finished our rehearsal dinner with a sing-along, ending with a rousing chorus of "Good-night, Sweetheart." The evening had ended just as I had imagined, with music and prayer. I kissed my future husband farewell, and we said good-night. I went back to my cottage, set out my shoes that fit perfectly, and thanked God that the next day I would be marrying the right man.

ideas to ponder

THE NIGHT BEFORE YOUR WEDDING IS NOT the time to try a new facial mask, a new shampoo, or over-the-counter sleeping pills! Don't overdo it. This is not the day to experiment. Don't push yourself to do the extra-heavy workout. This is a good time to surround yourself with comforting, familiar things such as your favorite music, your favorite bubble bath, your favorite slippers.

Set a bedtime for yourself and stick to it. The night before your wedding should be something you plan carefully and work hard to protect. It will be very easy to let those precious minutes of quiet time and sleep slip away if you're not committed to safeguarding them. The hours before you get married can be beautiful, sacred moments of reflection. It is also a time you can spend alone with God so He can prepare your heart for the marvelous work He will do tomorrow.

write it out

IMAGINE THE NIGHT BEFORE YOUR WEDDING:
a bath, a special phone call, an entry in your journal?
What are the things you could do to make it a very
special private time? Write them down. Remember
to allow yourself plenty of time to sleep.

_____

_____

_____

_____

_____

_____

_____

_____

_____

_____

_____

say it out loud

SPEAK THESE SCRIPTURES ALOUD BEFORE falling asleep.

> *Do not worry, saying, "What shall we eat?"*
> *or "What shall we drink?" or "What shall*
> *we wear?" . . . Indeed your Heavenly Father*
> *knows you need all these things. But seek ye*
> *first the kingdom of God and His righteousness*
> *and all these things will be added unto you.*
> *Therefore do not worry about tomorrow, for*
> *tomorrow will take care of itself. . . .*
>
> MATTHEW 6:31–34

> *I will lie down and sleep in peace, for You,*
> *O Lord, make me dwell in safety.*
>
> PSALM 4:8

IV

the big day

Here all seeking is over,
The lost has been found,
a mate has been found
to share the chills of winter—
now Love asks
that you be united.
Here is a place to rest,
A place to sleep,
a place in heaven.
Now two are becoming one,
the black night is scattered,
the eastern sky grows bright.
At last the great day has come!

HAWAIIAN SONG
from the translation of Craighill Handy and Mary Kawena Pukui
adapted by Jane Hirshfield

it's raining
and the police are
still here

I AWOKE THE MORNING OF MY WEDDING TO SEE THE rain pounding the balcony outside my window with such force that it was leaking into my bedroom. The thousands of square feet of tenting that had taken ten days to erect was in danger of collapsing. My Irish dream of walking to my wedding from the bridal cottage was disappearing as I watched a torrent of water and mud flow down the hill from the tents to my front door.

I learned that last night's fugitive was still at large and had most likely spent a miserable night hiding in the rain. Guests, caterers, florists, everyone coming in and out of the ranch were now being stopped and searched by the police. If the man wasn't apprehended soon, our wedding vows would be drowned out by the sound of police helicopters. Friends began to show up and offer their condolences, shaking their heads and clucking about the rain and the circumstances. But I had put it all in God's hands from the moment I'd gotten out of bed, so I just smiled and shrugged and went about my business. The only problem was, I had given myself too much business to do. There was a brunch to attend, there was a massage to get, there were bridesmaids' gifts to wrap, there was even a short music rehearsal for the cabaret to be held after the reception. Not to mention hair and make-up and getting dressed for a wedding.

FIVE MINUTES IN THE SHOWER AND OTHER MISTAKES

It wasn't until I hopped into the shower an hour and a half before the ceremony that I realized I had neglected to build into my schedule any quiet time for myself. Five minutes standing under hot water wasn't nearly enough time to stop and say to myself, "Hey, it's your wedding day! How do you feel? You'll want to remember all of this someday." Why hadn't I planned things so that I could have taken a leisurely bath, prayed one more time, maybe even written my impressions in a journal?

Jon was smart. He planned absolutely nothing for himself that day other than to visit with friends in the morning and spend the afternoon alone with his thoughts and with God. By five o'clock, the appointed hour for our nuptials, Jon was, if not totally relaxed, at least ready. If I had it to do over, I'd have done it his way.

I regret not stopping with my bridesmaids and hugging and getting a picture with each one before rushing out the door to get to the church on time.

And I fervently wish that I'd had a private moment with my mother before my wedding. She was in a wheelchair, and there wasn't time to get her behind the scenes where I was waiting. They wheeled her right into our makeshift chapel, and all I could do was peek through the curtain and see her from a distance. I wanted to connect with her, to look her in the eyes and to say, "Mommy, I love you. Thank you for everything." But somehow the time had just slipped away.

My advice to you, then, is to learn from my mistakes. Give yourself the gift of time. Your wedding day is not the day to feel rushed. Slow down. Press the Pause button. Take some deep breaths. Spend some time with God, spend time with your thoughts, and spend time with the people you love. You will cherish those memories much more than any extra time spent at the beauty salon. And you'll have a better chance of avoiding any last-minute disasters.

THE LAST ACT OF FAITH

Fifty minutes before the ceremony I got the news that our wedding "mascot," the tragic fugitive, had finally been arrested while attempting to sneak off the property in the trunk of a taxi he had summoned from a pay phone. We breathed a sigh of relief and shook our heads. One down, one to go. It was still raining.

The last minutes were packed with mascara and panty hose and earrings and loading on all the borrowed, blue, old, and new somethings. Suddenly it was 4:45 P.M., and my wedding was going to start in fifteen minutes. Time to put on the dress. Past time, in fact. We rushed into the other room where the dress hung from the bathroom door and suddenly I was gripped with terror. The dress was still hanging in the bag right where we had left it when it was delivered by the bridal shop two days earlier. I stared at it in the horrible realization that I had been so busy, I'd never taken the dress out of the bag to make sure they had sent the right one. I took a deep breath and started to unzip the bag, sending up a silent prayer: "Oh, Lord, please let it be the right dress. And the veil, let it be in there, too. Please, please, please. . . ."

Before the bag was open, I already had His answer: "The dress doesn't matter."

Suddenly I knew that if I had to, I could go down the aisle wearing jeans and a T-shirt, and I would still be marrying the right man in the presence of God, surrounded by the people who loved me. In that split second, I learned one more spiritual lesson. I realized that fifteen minutes from now, God would not be uniting a wedding dress and a tuxedo in holy matrimony. He would be performing a miracle with two naked human souls. What we wore on our bodies wasn't going to make any difference at all. I finished unzipping the bag. My dress was inside. So was the veil.

We buttoned all the buttons, took a last look in the mirror, and at the stroke of five, I stepped outside to get into the waiting van that would drive me up the hill to the wedding tent. But something was different. I looked around. The rain had stopped. I laughed out loud, I hitched up my wedding dress and walked to my wedding.

ideas to ponder

MAKE TWO "EMERGENCY KITS" FOR YOUR-self. One kit carries the essentials—aspirin, Band-Aids, a nail-mending kit, a sewing kit, spot remover, safety pins, perhaps even a cell phone. The other kit is a Spiritual Emergency Kit. It's your bible. Write on 3×5 cards the scriptures that have been most helpful to you since you began this process. Stop occasionally during the day and speak the words that have brought you peace in the past. It will be a familiar and com-forting reminder of all you and God have done to bring you to this moment.

Pack a special "dressing-for-the-ceremony" bag. Don't put *anything* in the bag other than what you'll be wearing. Put your underwear, your panty hose, your shoes, your slip, even your jew-elry all together in one place and have it packed a week ahead of time, before you have to scramble to pull it all together. This minimizes the risk of forgetting or losing something. Just looking at my prepacked bag gave me a tremendous sense of relief all week long. And predictably, I ended up dressing in a hurry and could never have pulled everything together from different bags so quickly.

write it out

WRITE THE SCHEDULE OF EVENTS FOR YOUR
wedding day.

_____

_____

_____

_____

Now go back over the schedule and find something
that isn't absolutely necessary.

_____

_____

_____

Now that you have made some time for yourself,
write down one or two things that you absolutely
don't want to forget to do on your wedding day.
Follow them up with a written commitment to make
them a priority.

_____

_____

_____

_____

say it out loud

Rejoice evermore. Pray without ceasing. In everything give thanks: for this is the will of God.

1 THESSALONIANS 5:16–18

Dear Lord,

The day has come, and, thanks to Your guidance and mercy, I am strong and renewed, cleansed and ready to come before the altar. Thank You for Your faithfulness and Your mercy. Thank You for bringing us through these weeks of planning. Thank You for being here today to bless our wedding. Father, in the hours to come, please help me to be constantly aware of Your presence and to reflect Your glory in my joy. Amid the excitement of the day, help me to recognize special memories as they occur and help me to hold on to them. Be with my fiancé right now as he prepares to meet me at the end of the aisle. Give him peace and joy and put Your arms around us as we stand together. My heart is so full, Lord, but I know that You know all that I want to say. I love You.

                                                            Amen.

23

the best thing
I did
on my wedding day

In the months before my wedding, I collected greeting cards of all sorts: beautiful wedding cards, funny wedding cards, blank cards, cards that reminded me of good memories or things to come. I made sure I had exactly the right number of cards so that I could send one to Jon every hour on our wedding day until the ceremony.

On the morning of our wedding, I wrote love letters to Jon, different thoughts to match each card. I wrote about my joy, my gratitude to God, my indifference to the rain, my love for him, and my excitement about the hours to come. I described my feelings as I counted down the hours until we would meet at the altar. I kept a few cards blank and wrote a few other notes as events triggered new thoughts during the day. Jon was delighted to receive the hourly dispatches, and he sent back notes of his own. It was easy to exchange so many cards, of course, because we were both staying in cottages on the same property, and friends were there to deliver them for us. But whether one letter or many are exchanged, a note to your beloved before your wedding is a precious gift.

What's so interesting is that I had never written a love letter to Jon before that day. It felt good to commit my thoughts and feelings about him and about our future together on paper, in my own words, before we said the same thing in our vows.

Jon later told me how much my messages meant to him. They arrived like clockwork to inspire his prayers and meditations on our special day. And they gave him something to anticipate each hour, making the day pass a little faster.

Now, Jon and I have a precious permanent record of what was going on in our minds and hearts in the hours before we became husband and wife. The messages read like journal entries, each one a freeze-frame of a particular moment that might have slipped from our memories as time went by. And I found myself saying things to him that I had never said before.

That was a revelation. Because of it, we started what we intend to continue as a lifelong exchange of written expressions of our love, our concerns, our hopes, and our prayers. We have a beautiful antique postbox that sits on a table just inside the entrance to our home. It is our private post office. Whenever the spirit moves us, we write notes for each other and drop them into the box. I never cease to get a thrill when I open the box and find a new note from Jon. And I take great comfort in scribbling, at odd moments, those thoughts of him and for him which might otherwise have gotten lost in the maelstrom of our busy lives.

It is as though we have two relationships. One is verbal and ephemeral, dependent entirely on what each of us remembers about what was said and how intently each of us was listening at any given moment. The other relationship is tangible, captured forever on paper. It constitutes irrefutable evidence of our love in words that can be studied and cherished and referred to again and again as our relationship grows richer and stronger with each passing year.

ideas to ponder

OUR "POST OFFICE" WAS INSPIRED BY A tradition my friend Jane and her husband have observed since they were married. They keep a journal in which they write to each other irregularly. She might write something to him on a page and then close the book. Then he'll come and find it that day, or two days later, or three days later, and he'll respond to her. Then at some point she'll open the book and keep the dialogue going. They started the journal right after they were married, and they now have many volumes. Jane told me that if there were ever a fire in their home, those books would be the only possessions she would try to save.

> *The holiest of all holidays are those*
> *Kept in silence and apart;*
> *The secret anniversaries of the heart.*
> HENRY WADSWORTH LONGFELLOW

Instead of store-bought cards to give to your fiancé on your wedding day, you could make your own by writing favorite verses from the scriptures on blank cards.

If you're not as familiar with the Bible as you'd like to be, why not get one with a concordance at the end. This is a sort of index, with topics arranged in alphabetical order, and relevant passages listed by book, chapter, and verse. You can look up key words such as *love, prayer,* and *marry,* and you'll be referred to verses that might speak to you and your fiancé on your wedding day and beyond.

Personally, I love the Psalms and the book of Philippians. They are good places to start or to get back into the habit of reading the Bible.

write it out

IF YOU SEE YOUR FIANCÉ JUST ABOUT EVERY day, you're probably not in the habit of writing to him. But the frequent words of love you say sometimes carry greater weight when you take the time to write them down. They can be read and reread and saved. Take this opportunity to let your fiancé know why you love him. Let him know that you thank God every day for him and for the love God has given you both.

_____

_____

_____

_____

_____

_____

_____

_____

_____

_____

24

God's favorite part

Down at your feet, Oh Lord,
Is the most high place
In your presence, Lord
We seek your face
We seek your face
For there is no higher calling
No greater honor than to bow
And kneel before your throne
I'm amazed at your glory
Embraced by your mercy
Oh, Lord, I live to worship You!

LENNY LEBLANC
AND GREG GULLEY
"No Higher Calling"

EVERYBODY HAS A FAVORITE PART WHENEVER THEY attend a wedding. For many people, it's seeing the bride go down the aisle. For others it's witnessing the couple's first kiss as husband and wife. I think perhaps mine was hearing Gwen's voice deliver this song of worship as Jon and I knelt to take our first communion together as husband and wife.

I suspect that God's favorite part is the whole ceremony itself, when He creates the altar where He transforms two into one. That's why you and your fiancé will want to plan it with care so that it reflects your spiritual beliefs, as it sets the tone for your married life.

WHO WILL PERFORM THE CEREMONY?

Jon and I were blessed with a pastor who takes the time to get to know each couple before performing their wedding ceremony, to tailor his words to their unique journey and affirm the steps they took to get to this moment. Most conscientious ministers, priests, rabbis, and other officiants are very much aware of the potential to allow one wedding to sound like all the others. Our own pastor acknowledged the temptation as he began our ceremony. "I have performed many marriages myself, and I find I've been vulnerable to simply going through the motions. . . . Long ago I began to ask the Lord what I could do to keep each marriage a distinct and separate thing in my spirit so that I don't become a kind of 'Marryin' Sam,' a preacher who recites a few lines, collects another five bucks, and sends people on their way. And so I pray on the morning of the wedding ceremony I am to perform, and I ask, 'Lord, give me a prophetic picture of this couple.' Because of what I believe about the Holy Spirit and His desire to fulfill promise in our lives, I also believe He wants to tell us in advance what He would like to do so that we will not attempt to achieve it ourselves, but rather open up to His power to perform it. I'd like to share what I received this morning from the Lord about you."

Pastor Hayford went on to tell us that he had received a clear image of two wax hearts melted and reformed into a single golden one. It seems like an obvious metaphor for a vision except that in our case, we had truly been through the fire; the years and months that preceded our nuptials did, in fact, involve a destruction of the "old" Martha and Jon in order to allow God to make us over according to His perfect plan for us. Many, many guests have since commented that Pastor Hayford's story of the two wax hearts melted into gold was the most emotional moment of the ceremony.

It is my hope that you, too, will find a committed spiritual leader who will take the time as Pastor Hayford did to ask God to guide him or her and to reveal a unique and blessed way to make your wedding, and ultimately your union, unlike any other.

THE VOWS

Are your vows realistic? I have heard some frankly impractical vows. Can you actually promise "I will never disappoint you"? "I will never hurt you"? "I will always tell you the truth"? As much as we want to try to live up to these things, we are human. Don't think that just saying the vows automatically enables you to keep them.

It says in the Bible that it is better not to make a vow to God than to make one and break it. And remember this: You are not just making a vow to your beloved; you have asked God to be the third strand in the marriage braid that is being woven this day, and your vows to each other are vows made with Him as well. They constitute a contract among all of you, so make sure you plan to live up to what you actually promise. Commit to your love, commit to support and stand by each other *even if* there is disappointment or pain or failure. That's what love is anyway, not that you will be the perfect spouse, but that you will be a loving and constant spouse.

It's so easy to be caught up in the moment that your vows can fly by and you won't remember what you have said. So promise yourself to truly listen to each other. And make sure you get a copy of your vows to reread later. It would be wonderful to have them at the end of the night to repeat to each other privately.

FOREVER HOLD YOUR PEACE?

As I mentioned earlier, many people choose to eliminate the charge: "If any man can show just cause why these two may not lawfully be joined together, let him now speak or hereafter hold his peace." It recalls an era when a woman was considered property and the inquiry referred to whether the properties were going to be justly distributed. Because of this, Jon and I did not include it in our service. However, it is still included in many ceremonies and can be used for a very different and effective purpose. I also will always remember a moment in a wedding which was performed by Della Reese who plays the angel Tess on *Touched By An Angel* and is also an ordained minister. Della stood with her back to the congregation and had the bride and groom facing her and their guests. When the time came, Della delivered the charge but waited a long time after "forever hold your peace," as if she were expecting an answer.

Not surprisingly, there was silence in the church. But Della didn't go on. She turned around very slowly and gave the eagle eye to everybody in the room. We all chuckled uncomfortably. Then Della said, "You have chosen not to speak. Continue to do so; you've just given up your right to speak in this marriage. This is no joke. This is serious. This is a private estate. If you have any problem with these people getting married, this was your time to speak. Whatever happens from this moment on is now between these two people and God."

Suddenly the words we had heard over and over at wedding after wedding had real meaning for all of us. It was a wedding moment I have never forgotten because it forced me to realize that I, as a guest and a friend, have the power to contribute or detract from a marriage. At that moment, I determined to honor and support this couple in a way that I had not considered before.

MAKE A JOYFUL NOISE UNTO THE LORD!

As you plan your ceremony, please be sure to take plenty of time to plan the music. Many couples don't consider themselves very musical, and they tend to leave the music decisions to others. They might have some favorite tunes or a particular musical style such as rock and roll or swing that they would like to hear at the reception, but many times the music during the actual ceremony is not given much attention.

Invest a few evenings listening to music, and researching the names of classical or sacred pieces that you have heard and enjoyed in your life.

There is a tremendously gratifying feeling when you hear favorite and old familiar tunes as you are being married. It provides a comforting generational sense of the cycle of life. I chose to begin the service with the first song I ever learned to sing, "Jesus Loves Me (This I Know, for the Bible Tells Me So.) It was a special message I arranged to send to myself moments before I walked down the aisle to remind me of all that had gone on before and to remember to keep a childlike wonder of all that was ahead. Hymns that your grandmother used to sing, music you played in your high-school orchestra, or a praise song you sing with Bible-study friends can be a sweet and private way to remember and honor some of your guests. To me, one of the most moving moments of our ceremony was when our choir of family and friends sang "Let Us Break Bread Together." It had been the traditional closing song of my high school Concert Choir. Some of those choir members were singing that day and other high-school friends were sitting in the congregation. Although I couldn't see them, I knew what all of us were thinking at that moment, and there was a great sense of communion.

When you ask friends and relatives to participate in the actual service, beware of what I call "giving your wedding away." In your eagerness to include loved ones in your ceremony, don't get into the position of allowing others to use this as an opportunity to "show off their talent." I went to one wedding in which the groom completed his vows, picked up a microphone, and began to sing a love song. The problem was, he couldn't sing on key. On top of that, he was clearly playing to the audience and did not even look at his bride. I don't question his love for her, but he didn't have the experience to pull off what should have been a truly intimate moment. Instead it became a strange performance that made the rest of us uncomfortable. A wedding is not a talent showcase.

On the other hand, if you have truly talented friends whose music will be a contribution rather than a performance, their gift can be a memorable blessing. One remarkable friend of ours is a composer, and in the minutes before her ceremony began, her gifted friends performed many of the love songs she has written. It was marvelous preparation for the ceremony and a lovely insight into her heart. Our dear friends Randy and Elizabeth Travis came a great distance to attend our wedding and to bring the gift of Randy's music. Randy sang a simple and moving "Amazing Grace" at the end of our service, and many guests told us later that it hadn't even registered that they were listening to a country-music superstar, because it was a natural and organic part of the service. My sister sang, Randy sang, my school pals sang; it wasn't a concert, it was a family event.

There are many ways to bring beautiful music into your ceremony without relying on the traditional organ music. A piano coupled with a single guitar, a cello, a flute, or a harp can be elegant and effective and less expensive than a string quartet. Even a well-made audiotape of recorded music is preferable, in my mind, to no music at all. Music simply has the ability to soften hearts and prepare them for blessings. Below you'll find some of our favorite wedding music:

PEACEFUL PRE-CEREMONY
Canon in D by Pachelbel
"Water Music" by Handel
"Sheep May Safely Graze" by Bach
"Jesu, Joy of Man's Desiring" by Bach
"Lo, How a Rose E'er Blooming"
"Surely the Presence of the Lord Is in This Place"
"Greensleeves"

PROCESSIONALS
"Bridal March" from *Lohengrin* by Wagner
"The Trumpet Voluntaire" by Purcell
"A Mighty Fortress Is Our God" by Luther

RECESSIONALS
"Wedding March" from *A Midsummer Night's Dream* by
    Mendelssohn
"Ode to Joy" from the Ninth Symphony by Beethoven

Trumpet Tune in C by Purcell
"All Hail the Power of Jesus' Name"
"God of Grace and God of Glory"

FAVORITE HYMNS
"Majesty"
"Great Is Thy Faithfulness"
"Amazing Grace"
"There's a Sweet, Sweet Spirit in This Place"
"Take My Hand, Precious Lord"
"Great Is the Lord"
"For the Beauty of the Earth"
"All Creatures of Our God and King"
"Blest Be the Tie That Binds"
"We Gather Together"
"It Is Well with My Soul (When Peace Like a River)"
"This Is My Father's World"
"His Name Is Wonderful"

Occasionally a couple will invite their guests to sing a hymn together as part of the service. If there are no hymnals, the lyrics are printed in the program. It is a very pleasant way for friends to contribute to the "sealing" process. Those who do not sing will certainly follow along in their programs and add their good thoughts. A hymn by the congregation can have a secondary benefit of relaxing and coalescing the group before the reception.

The revival of interest in ethnic music has yielded some especially beautiful music. Couples with ties to Israel, Ireland, Mexico, Polynesia, the Caribbean, Eastern Europe, etc., have a rich musical heritage from which to draw unique musical pieces.

We recently attended a beautiful wedding in which the Chinese family of the groom joined with the Scottish family of the bride to present a remarkable mix of bagpipes and Chinese toasts and American tradition.

Be sure to go over your musical choices with your officiant to confirm their appropriateness. Rabbis, for example, often take exception to the use of Wagner's *Lohengrin* due to the composer's documented anti-Semitism. Similarly, they may reject Mendelssohn's Wedding March, citing his rejection of his Jewish faith. And many conservative churches will often disallow the use of secular music during the ceremony.

DO YOU (CLICK!) TAKE THIS (CLICK!) . . . ?

Yes, you want to have pictures of your wedding. But don't let the photographer turn the ceremony into a media circus of popping flashbulbs and clicking shutters. And if you choose to videotape the service, make sure the videographer doesn't become a director. He's there to capture your wedding, not to stage it. The cameras should be set up discreetly, perhaps behind flower arrangements, so that they aren't focal points when people enter the sanctuary. Also, please don't let the guys with the cameras wander up and down the aisle. The resulting noise and distraction are not worth the pictures you might get. Let the holiness of the ceremony prevail. Jon and I did not allow any photographs to be taken during the ceremony. There is one of me as I enter and one of us as we leave, but in between it remained a very private service uninterrupted by clicks and flashes.

STARTING A TRADITION

Your wedding is the perfect time to establish customs you'll cherish throughout your married life. When Della Reese performs marriage ceremonies, she often says to the bride and groom, "Remember how you feel in this place at this moment. In times of challenge, you can always come back to this moment when he is the greatest man in the world to you and she is what you have already dreamed come true. When you face those challenges, this is the place, this is the love you will come back to." Wise counsel indeed. One sure way to make the mental and spiritual journey back to the moment when you became husband and wife is to create traditions that will bring the memories to life. Here are some examples:

The Unity Candle

This is a lovely way to symbolize the creation of a new family. The parents of the bride and the parents of the groom light separate candles. Then the bride and groom combine the two flames by simultaneously lighting a larger candle representing the union of the couple. Treasure that candle and light it as each anniversary rolls around. You might also want to light the candle whenever you need a renewal of your faith and your vows. For example, the candle can help you celebrate life events such as the birth of a child. It can also keep you on an even keel when you face disagreements or find yourselves coping with troubles. Lighting the candle can literally become the place where you return to find your love.

The Memory Box

Collect mementos from your wedding day and keep them in a pretty little chest, perhaps one engraved with your names and your wedding date. You might want to save the handkerchief you carried, a dried rose or two from your bouquet, the scripture cards from your Spiritual Emergency Kit, the love notes you wrote to your fiancé before the ceremony, the ribbon bouquet from your showers, a copy of your vows, and the handwritten notes your pastor or rabbi made for your ceremony. One thing I particularly enjoy are the RSVP cards that were returned with special notes written on them, such as "We will be there with bells on!!!" These and other souvenirs will jog memories that are even more vivid than the ones called up by simply looking at your wedding pictures. There is something about the very tactile process of going through a box of mementos that can recreate the feeling of being there. The scent of the day clings to them. Holding them and seeing them again is a powerful experience that can revive the memories and the sense of God's presence that you and your husband shared on your day of days.

The Communion Cup

If you are Christians, you may choose to take communion at your wedding. Jon and I did, although we decided not to invite our guests to partake because many of them are of different faiths. Pastor Hayford simply spoke to the congregation and explained the significance of communion as Jon and I served each other from the bread and the cup. We had lots of fun searching unusual shops and antique stores until we found the perfect communion cup. It was handmade by a Greek silversmith who had learned his trade from his father and grandfather on the island of Corfu. He was honored when he heard how we planned to use the beautiful cup he had designed. Jon and I used it to serve each other during the ceremony, and we use the cup during our private devotions at home to serve each other again and again. Every time we do this, we seek God's guidance and we ask Him to bless our union and keep it strong.

DON'T LET YOUR VOWS BE FORGOTTEN

You may want to have your vows copied by a calligrapher and then get them framed. Hang them in a prominent place in your home. They will be a regular reminder of the promises you made together in the presence of God.

Jon and I read our vows often, and I find that at least once a day I say to myself the part which goes, "I desire to become all that God wants me to be for you." One reason I have found repeating the vows to be so valuable is that as time goes by, they become more meaningful than ever. The simple words that we spoke to begin our life together have since become cornerstones of our marriage.

ideas to ponder

I SAW SOMETHING AT A WEDDING IN WASH-
ington, D.C., that I wish we had done at ours.
Instead of asking the arriving guests to sign a
guest book, the bride had placed small white
linen cards on a table near the entrance to the
sanctuary. Rather than just a signature, friends
wrote words of love and greetings and dropped
them into a basket. Later, all the cards were
pasted into a beautiful book. What I especially
loved about this as a guest was that I could take a
card and think about what I wanted to say and
drop it into the basket anytime rather than feel
rushed to sign just to let others in line behind
me have their turn.

write it out

WHETHER OR NOT YOU DECIDE TO WRITE YOUR
own vows, there are certainly things that you want to
be sure are said or not said in your ceremony. It was
important to us that everyone understood that we
had, by the grace of God alone, come to the altar as
two people changed and ready for a new life. Write
below what you want to be sure is included in your
vows or the remarks by your officiant.

say it out loud

THERE IS A BEAUTIFUL JEWISH PRAYER
that is always spoken at the beginning of a hol-
iday or a special season that is appropriate to
offer on a wedding day at the beginning of a
new life together. It is called the *Shehechyanu*. It
translates roughly like this:

> *Blessed art thou, O Lord, our God*
> *King of the universe,*
> *Who has kept us alive, sustained us and*
> *Brought us to this wonderful new season.*

Perhaps you already know this in Hebrew. Or
you can learn this simple prayer of praise in En-
glish. But practice it now, and speak it not only
on your wedding day but as you celebrate all the
seasons of your life.

a reception means
to receive

Jon and I made a point of spending at least a few significant moments with each and every person at our reception. We wanted to create a welcoming atmosphere and let everyone know how glad we were that they had taken the time out of their busy lives to celebrate with us. Here are the strategies we used to be sure we were available for our guests and also to put everyone at ease. Remember, a reception means to receive, and your guests are there to give you their love and blessings, and it's important to graciously make time and effort to accept them.

CELEBRATE AND REGULATE

We had a program printed for our reception that let people know what to expect. This was very important to me because I've been to many a lovely wedding that was marred, for example, by outspoken guests proposing inappropriate toasts. Worse than that, some guests pull pranks such as "stealing the bride" or handcuffing the groom. Not that we expected pranks to occur at our wedding, but a program nevertheless set the tone for the evening, and guests felt more comfortable when they knew what was coming.

DON'T ASK GUESTS TO DRIVE TOO FAR TO THE RECEPTION

We held our reception within walking distance from the sanctuary. My maid of honor, Robin, who had a garden wedding, did the same thing, and it was wonderful. If you have to choose between a grand ballroom and a simpler setting that's closer to the church or synagogue, I'd go with the latter. People may not want to spend an hour fighting traffic before they can relax and enjoy themselves.

THE RECEIVING LINE

There is a better way to receive your friends' good wishes than by asking them to stand and wait in a line for more than fifteen minutes. We chose not to have a receiving line at all because we had a fairly large guest list. It was more important to us to get people to their tables. Jon and I then took the opportunity to move from table to table during dinner. We also made sure our own table was in a spot that everyone could find easily. If you do decide to have a receiving line, consider having drinks and hors d'oeuvres served as people stand and wait.

At our reception, the first item on the program was a blessing before dinner sent by Roma Downey, who was unable to attend. It was delivered by our friend John Dye, the charming "Andrew" on *Touched By An Angel*. After that came the toasts, a heartfelt memory from Robin, a touching tribute from Jon's son, Christian, and his friend John Dellaverson, and a hilarious but tasteful roast by "Angel" producer Bob Colleary. Finally, Jon surprised and delighted all of us when he dedicated his toast to "the woman who changed my life—Martha's mother!"

We had a schedule for serving the food and beverages, and we offered the champagne as people entered, because generally

people will indulge in fewer mixed drinks if they've started off with champagne. Incidentally, if you have religious or addictive issues with alcohol, you may certainly choose not to serve alcohol at all. That is your prerogative. Don't feel pressured to do otherwise.

It may sound a bit rigid to literally schedule the evening, but remember that your guests should never be aware of a schedule at all. However, if your caterers and musicians and other workers are working without a schedule, then everyone will *definitely* notice.

THE SEATING PLAN

We started our seating plan by placing at each table a person who would be coming alone and who wouldn't know many other guests. Then we put our most gregarious and charming friends next to the ones who might need a little help in feeling included and comfortable. After that, we added to every table an interesting mix of ages and occupations. We did not always put people next to their friends. The result was lively conversation, new friendships, and a warm feeling of camaraderie for all.

THE DESERT ISLAND

Jon and I had a table all to ourselves. For one thing, this solved the problem of trying to decide who out of all our family and friends would be seated at the head table. Since no one sat with us, no one felt left out. But the most important reason for our "desert island" was that we wanted some private moments to connect and to reflect on the miracle of our brand-new union. I had our table set with cherished and familiar items—our own crystal champagne flutes, the cups we had picked out and used together, a bouquet of our favorite flowers. Think about what items would give meaning to your private table at your reception. Are there heirlooms such as your grandmother's china that you've loved since you were a little girl? Do you have a vase that once held roses he gave to you? Do you have a favorite framed photo of the two of you?

Also at your table, have a small blank journal and a pen. I know you'll be busy, but in random moments, jot down thoughts that occur to you, maybe even only a word or two that describes your mood. Record sweet things people say when they stop by to offer good wishes, these and anything at all you wouldn't want to forget. That way the memories won't fade as time goes by. Don't allow the journal to become an obligation. If you have written only a sentence by night's end, you'll still treasure what you wrote fifty years from now.

PHOTOGRAPHS ON THE TABLE

At the reception of our friends Kim and David, every table had pictures of the bride and groom from childhood on. They were great conversation starters and gave us all a tender and misty-eyed sense of how "swiftly go the years," as the song "Sunrise, Sunset" from *Fiddler on the Roof* reminds us.

CAMERAS ON THE TABLE

Some brides place disposable cameras on every table and ask guests to take photographs. That's a wonderful idea. But I didn't want my guests to feel obligated to click away instead of enjoying the food and one another's company. I also didn't want to spoil the lovely place settings at the table. The solution was to put lots of cameras in a big basket and let guests know that they could use them if they wanted. Some people had a great time snapping candids, and plenty of other people opted out of camera duty without feeling guilty. It's a great lifesaver for shy guests who welcome something to do.

THE MARRIAGE CERTIFICATE
AND THE FAMILY BIBLE

Instead of proposing by kneeling and asking me to marry him, Jon bought a huge leather-bound Bible. He gave it to me one night and said, "I'd like to put our names in this someday." And so when the day came that we could finally fill out that Bible's special page, it was particularly personal for us. We also had a replica designed by a calligrapher and asked our attendants and pastor to sign it on the night we were married. It now hangs in a frame in our house. You may want to have a beautiful wedding certificate available to be signed at the same time your witnesses sign your wedding license. There are a number of calligraphers who specialize in designing these, or you can find them in stationery or religious bookstores.

THE PHOTOGRAPHER IS NOT GOD

We stopped for what couldn't have been more than ten minutes to have our formal pictures taken while the guests were finding their tables. We were not missed and the reception was not delayed. And I'll tell you something: The formal pictures are disappointing because they are so posed. The photographs I cherish are the candid shots that capture special, natural moments of spontaneity and joy.

However, if the formal pictures mean a lot to you, find a solution that doesn't involve keeping people waiting forever. Two of my friends, Robin and Marilyn, had their pictures taken before their weddings. Robin arranged to have all the pictures taken in advance with the exception of the bride and groom together and this allowed her to still avoid seeing her husband until the ceremony. Once the reception got going, they slipped away to a nearby tree and had their formal shot taken together, and everyone had the pleasure of watching it happen. Marilyn and her husband, Jeff, agreed that it was more important to get their formal photos out of the way before the ceremony. Staying apart was not as important to them as keeping the momentum going from ceremony to reception. Jeff was still amazed to see Marilyn make her smashing entrance in her gown as he waited in the garden with his groomsmen. In some ways it was even better than waiting for her to walk down the aisle because he could tell her right away how very beautiful she was. It also gave them the added sense that they were now going into the ceremony together as a team.

THE WEDDING NIGHT

A few random thoughts about the wedding night. Customs have changed over the years. It used to be a great faux pas to leave the wedding before the bride and groom had retired. Today, wedding parties are known to go late into the night, and sometimes the bride and groom are the last to leave. So be considerate of those whose old-fashioned manners won't allow them to depart before you and encourage them to leave if they need to.

Arrange for a late-night dinner to be waiting for the two of you in your hotel room or wherever you plan to spend your wedding night. You will most likely be unaware of how much energy you have spent that day and will possibly find yourself rather hungry. A light, intimate meal will also be a nice way to unwind together.

If there are any tricks to getting you into your wedding dress, there will be tricks to getting you out! Don't just let someone else dress you that day without telling you what you need to unpin, unhook, and unbutton to shed your dress and protect it later, particularly if you will end the day in a different room from where you began.

Don't push yourself or your husband to create a passionate night after such a strenuous and frankly stressful day. Don't feel pressured to live up to a romantic scenario on your wedding night if you're just too tired. Making love is all about emotional energy, and you've been doing nothing but expending that for days.

Remember that scent and chemistry play a great part in the attraction between two people. So, while for you the new scent commemorates an important moment, one that you will be reminded of each time you wear it, your husband might feel differently. Men seem particularly sensitive to changes like that in women. Whether he knows why or not, a man will be somewhat disconcerted if the familiar scent of his mate has changed, which is surely not how you want him to feel on your special day.

ideas to ponder

WATCH YOUR CONSUMPTION OF ALCOHOL at the reception. It's natural to want to relax at the reception after the intensity of the ceremony has passed. But if you're mixing and greeting and dancing, chances are you won't be eating very much during the reception, and alcohol on an empty stomach could be disastrous.

An informal reception is a wonderful opportunity to create a truly relaxed family atmosphere. Encourage guests to bring guitars and get a sing-along going. We had a more formal reception in the early evening that retired to a nearby cigar room where the die-hards played guitar and sang old standards in a jam session that lasted late into the night. Is there a barbershop quartet in the room? Invite them to croon a tune or two. A nice way to honor your parents is to arrange to have "their song" played. Give them the spotlight, and then imagine yourselves twenty or thirty years from now as you watch them dance together.

This Irish toast to us from Roma Downey is a beautiful blessing that one of your guests may want to offer on your wedding day:

May you have warm words on a cold evening,
a full moon on a dark night,
and the road downhill all the way to your door.
May you be poor in misfortune,
rich in blessings, slow to make enemies,
quick to make friends.
But rich or poor, quick or slow,
may you know nothing but happiness
from this day forward.

write it out

TRY TO RECALL THE BEST WEDDING RECEPTION you ever attended. Do you remember it because it was elegant or just a lot of fun? Was it special because you met interesting people or because the bride and groom had spent memorable moments with you? I remember feeling very special at a wedding simply because the bride insisted on having her picture taken with me. Write down the "little things" that have made for a successful reception that you would like to repeat.

_____

_____

_____

_____

_____

_____

_____

_____

_____

_____

_____

say it out loud

IT'S EASY TO FORGET ABOUT GOD ONCE the party has started, but remember that when you invited Him to the wedding, He came for the whole thing. Take a moment at your private table to say a quiet prayer together to thank God for your beautiful ceremony and to ask Him to bless and infuse the night to come with genuine celebration and rejoicing.

V

the day
after
your wedding

This is the day which the Lord hath made;
we will rejoice and be glad in it.

PSALM 118:24

26

good morning!

*Let your lives overflow
with thanksgiving for all
He has done.*

COLOSSIANS 2:7

DON'T SET THE ALARM. THE DAY AFTER YOUR WEDDING is one day when you deserve to wake up slowly, say a prayer together, and enjoy the dawn of your life as husband and wife. This might even be the time to consummate your marriage. If you were too exhausted last night—and that's quite understandable—consider how joyous it could be to wake up refreshed and ready to give a full measure of love and emotional energy to the man who is now and forever your husband.

Jon and I chose not to hurry off on a honeymoon right after the wedding, partly because we knew we'd be tired but also because so many of our guests came from far away. We knew they would be staying the night, and we wanted to see them one more time. We invited anyone interested to join us in a brief, non-denominational Sunday service the next morning in our temporary "church" before the tent was taken down. We were amazed at how many guests of every faith showed up. Some of them brought guitars, and we sang a few hymns together. Old friends offered prayers and dedicated songs to us, and our do-it-yourself worship service was a relaxed and spontaneous group effort.

Immediately following, we held a wedding breakfast in the nearby garden. It was a happy, relaxed, chatty get-together, and the guests found it easy to strike up a conversation with someone they recognized from the reception the night before. The sense of a shared miracle created a family feeling among the guests, and many commented on how nice it was to see us now as a married couple. They shared a fun sense of "accomplishment," having all taken part in the "before" and now in the "after."

The best moment of all was when my mother finally sang. She may have been too choked up to deliver "The Lord's Prayer" during the ceremony but by the time the breakfast rolled around, she was ready to warble. With me right beside her wheelchair, she gave us a heartfelt rendition of "You Are My Sunshine" that inspired everyone to join in. What a wonderful memory to cherish from the first day of my married life.

ideas to ponder

THE FIRST DAY OF YOUR MARRIAGE IS A happy, hopefully relaxed day, in which you can stop planning and simply "be." Consider a few suggestions on how to spend your day:

Take some time to compare your impressions of the wedding while they are still fresh. Surely your recollections will be similar in some ways and vastly different in others.

Look through your guest book, or if your guests wrote special messages on individual cards, read them together. This would also be a good time to collect your little mementos for your memory box before they are scattered or lost.

Consider taking a day to recover before rushing off to catch a plane and "start" your honeymoon. It has a better chance of being all you hope it to be if it begins with peace.

write it out

SO MUCH TIME AND CREATIVITY CAN BE SPENT planning all the events for a wedding, sometimes the day after can get forgotten. Take a moment to imagine the First Day of your marriage. How would it begin? How would you spend the day? How would it end? Write it out.

_____

_____

_____

_____

_____

_____

_____

_____

_____

_____

_____

_____

_____

_____

_____

say it out loud

Dear God,

It says in Proverbs 4:18 that "the path of the just is as the shining light that shineth more and more unto the perfect day." Thank You for the dawn of this first day of our married life and for all the days to come. We are blessed that You were present at our wedding to sanctify and justify our union, and we are at peace knowing that You shall be the bright and shining Presence in our marriage now and forever.

Amen.

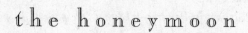

the honeymoon

Be still and know that I am God.
PSALM 46:10

You've just been glued together. You need some time to let the glue set. In some earlier cultures this concept was embraced so seriously that couples were released from work and all responsibility for an entire year to help them adjust to each other as husband and wife. That's not realistic today, but it's a great idea—an acknowledgment of how sacred and vital the beginning of a marriage is not only to the couple but to society. A year off may not be an option in this country, but even if all you can manage is a few days away, do all you can to escape society's demands long enough to let the realization of what you have done sink in. It's a hard thing to explain until you've done it, but you simply *need* each other and no one else during the early days and weeks of your marriage. It's as if your marriage is your first child and you need to nurture it and protect it from the outside world until it's ready to stand alone.

Remember, too, that your honeymoon is not so much a dream trip as it is a chance to find some peace. Don't make it one of those six-cities-in-six-days whirlwind vacations. For one thing, unless you and your husband are seasoned globetrotters, and unless you already know that you get along just fine even when you're road-weary or jet-lagged, this is not the time to discover how to be good traveling companions. Make your honeymoon all about each other, not about trekking through museums or dashing to make plane connections in unfamiliar airports.

Also, agree on a clear budget and stick to it. There's a tendency to go a little crazy when you're away from your regular routines even if you're usually conservative with money. You don't want to start married life with a whopping credit-card bill.

I had always envisioned going to Paris on my honeymoon or taking a Mediterranean cruise or perhaps even going to Fiji. But we only had five days off, and we didn't want to spend most of that precious time traveling. Our plan was to go to the Post Ranch Inn at Big Sur in Northern California because we loved the ocean and the inn offered exquisite views and absolute solitude, no televisions allowed. But the same torrential rains that threatened our wedding managed to wipe out the roads to Big Sur, and we never made it to our honeymoon beach house. The kind folks at the San Ysidro Ranch where we had held the wedding allowed us to stay in our charming wedding-night cottage the rest of the week. It wasn't what we had planned, but, like everything else at our wedding, it was what we needed. We didn't have to pack again, or travel again. We simply stayed put and relaxed. It was perfect.

We let the glue set. We're both very glad we did.

ideas to ponder

DON'T FORGET TO INVITE GOD TO THE honeymoon. Begin every morning with an invitation for Him to add His blessing to whatever you choose to do. Your honeymoon may be a skiing trip or a long drive through the redwoods or a camping adventure in the canyons of Utah. Perhaps it's going to be a few quiet days on the coast of Maine or at a bed-and-breakfast in Wisconsin. Whatever you choose to do, whether you are hiking and water skiing or just reading books and going to dinner, don't forget that God helped to make your wedding meaningful. He can do the same with your honeymoon.

write it out

WRITE DOWN YOUR IDEAS FOR A DREAM HONEY-
moon. Ask your fiancé to do the same. Be sure to
consider your time limitations and travel time on both
ends of your trip. Now compare your lists and decide
on a plan that suits you both. Then make a realistic
budget that won't strain your resources.

_____

_____

_____

_____

_____

_____

_____

_____

_____

_____

_____

_____

_____

_____

say it out loud

Dear God,

Grant us the wisdom to take time away from the demands of our busy lives so that we may focus on our newly formed union and begin our marriage by making it our priority in life. And, Lord, help our love and our sense of adventure to continue to grow even when our honeymoon is over.

Amen.

28

and now it begins

*The steadfast love of the Lord never
ceases, his mercies never come to an
end. They are new every morning.*
LAMENTATIONS 3:22,23

THE WEDDING IS OVER, THE HONEYMOON IS A MEMORY,
and now it all begins, the rest of your life with the man you love.

It has been a privilege to share some spiritual wedding
lessons with you, and it is my sincerest prayer that you have
found some encouragement and inspiration in these pages. Jon
and I know that we don't have all the answers, but just as the
angels have done on our show, we know how to point "up" to
the One who does.

Our marriage is relatively new to us, too. It has been a glorious journey so far, and the honeymoon shows no signs of ending. I like to think that's what God had in mind when He
accepted the invitation to our wedding; He wanted to bring a
gift that would create not just one sacred day in our lives, but
would support our marriage with His grace and love all the rest
of our days, too.

There is still much for us to learn about marriage, but of one
thing I am already certain. There was a bond created between

the three of us that day. It was the cord of three strands that I spoke of earlier. It keeps me and Jon and our Lord drawn tightly together through the peaceful days, the glorious days, the fun days. And if Jon or I have a difficult day, if tempers are short or patience is running low or misunderstandings cause pain, then the Lord is there, too, to draw the strands even tighter.

One of the most popular scriptures in the Bible comes from the first book of Corinthians and it is often read at wedding ceremonies.

> *Love is patient; love is kind; love is not envious or boastful*
> *or arrogant or rude. Love does not insist on its own way;*
> *it is not irritable or resentful; it does not rejoice in wrong-*
> *doing, but rejoices in the truth. It bears all things, hopes all*
> *things, endures all things. Love never fails.*
>
> 1 CORINTHIANS 13:4–8

I have always read this passage with a certain distance. The love described here seems impossible to achieve all the time, "never failing." I have never known any human being who was always patient, always kind, never jealous, and never irritable. And so, in a marriage without God, when things get tough you can only hope that if one is down, the other will be up. But if the day comes that you're both down, who will lift you up then? When one fails another with anger or unkindness, the other's natural reaction is to withdraw in pain and confusion. How easily things can unravel after that, especially if we rely only on ourselves to have all the necessary wisdom and love to keep it together.

But if we have both put our faith in Someone beyond ourselves, then whenever the problem *is* ourselves, there is a saving grace and a saving place to go. It is to God, the third strand in the marriage we established together.

> For we know only in part, and we prophesy in part, but
> when the complete comes, the partial will come to an end.
> When I was a child, I spoke like a child, I thought like a
> child, I reasoned like a child. When I became an adult, I put
> an end to childish ways. For now we see in a mirror dimly,
> but then we will see face to face. Now I know only in part,
> then I will know fully, even as I have been fully known.
> And now faith, hope, and love abide, these three, and the
> greatest of these is love.
>
> 1 CORINTHIANS 13:9–13

Most people don't spend a lot of time on the last verses of the "love chapter" in 1 Corinthians because at first glance they are not easy to understand. But they actually provide the very crucial answer to the questions, "How can I love like that? How can love never fail if I'm human and fail myself?" The answer comes in the last line. Because even when faith wavers and hope falters, love has the power to restore them both. Not the human, imperfect kind of love, but God's love. The perfect kind. And that's the kind of love that will hold anything together.

The truth is, things will change. That is certain. Nothing God has ever created on earth was designed to stay the same. Only His faithfulness and His love remain constant. Just as we grow from childhood to become adults and see the world as it really is, there will come a time when we will grow from a simple understanding of love to a more complete one.

But you have already begun that process. You have stepped out in faith and invited God to your wedding in the hope that

He would come with the gifts you needed to create a meaning-ful wedding *and* a lasting marriage. In the process of delivering this gift, He may have asked you to do things that didn't always make sense. But someday, they will. If you have put your life and your marriage into His hands, then He holds every day of them there, too. He knows what is ahead, and He knows how to get you through it together with Him.

If you're like me, you probably received a lot of advice about marriage before your wedding. I remember two pieces of wis-dom in particular that I have taken to heart. First, our friends Karen and Jim made us promise to pray with each other every day. With few exceptions, we have begun every morning prais-ing God, thanking Him for the gift of brand-new mercy that He pours into each new day, and turning over to Him whatever the next twenty-four hours will bring. The prayers are long or short, sometimes tearful or joyful. But the day is always better, and we are always stronger if we have stopped to "check the cord" and put all three strands into place.

My second piece of good advice came from Della Reese. She took me aside after we announced our engagement and said simply, "It's a new day, every day. Wake up every morning and thank God for your wonderful man and ask God what you can do to make your husband happy." It was a simple yet priceless gift. It's not about sacrifice or subservience. It's about power. I have been entrusted by God with the power to be the one per-son in the world who can make my husband really happy day after day after day. And when I do that, I am happy, too. A note, a phone call, coffee brewing in the kitchen, a song he loves to hear, his favorite meal, a good conversation. These little daily gifts are the evidence of our respect for each other as well as our love.

When I was growing up, my father always rose very early and had breakfast before my mother was awake. Every morning, for nearly fifty years, he would make coffee and read the newspaper quietly in the kitchen, waiting for her to awaken. Often I would sit with him before I walked to school. Only years later did I realize that Daddy never just poured a cup for himself; there was always another empty cup and saucer sitting beside the coffee pot, set for my mother. Every day, in a simple, quiet act, he found a way to say, "I'm here. I'm thinking of you. I love you." Surely there were days of frustration or disagreement. But never once was that coffee cup absent from the kitchen counter. No matter what the current challenge, love was always waiting there.

What you have just read are the words I wrote ten years ago, as a bride. Even as I wrote those words, I wondered if they would still apply ten years later. The answer is *yes*. The honeymoon may be over, but the marriage only seems to be deeper and richer than I imagined. We have taken the occasional "second honeymoon," we have celebrated twelve anniversaries, watched the video tape, re-read our vows, and continued to pray together.

We have also hit the inevitable bumps in the road—disagreement, illness, career and financial ups and downs, not to mention the daily challenge of responsible parenting. I am happy to say that we are a happy family; whatever the bumps have been in the road, we have stayed *on* the road. Our journey through this life continues to be guided by love. It began by inviting God to take the trip with us, and we hold onto the promise that love will be there when He brings us home.

Love, indeed, never fails. Not when the God who knows no failure is the Source of your love. It is always there to draw from; it is always there to supply strength and joy and peace. It is God, and He loves you and your husband so much. He loves you so much that He will come to your wedding when you invite Him. So much that He will stay for your marriage. So much. God bless you and keep you now and forever.

As for me and my house, we will serve the Lord.
JOSHUA 24:15

VI

a few words
TO
men from
Jon

For I know the plans I have for you," declares the Lord,
"plans to prosper you and not to harm you,
plans to give you a hope and a future.
JEREMIAH 29:11

be thou a blessing

I ACCEPTED THE INVITATION TO WRITE THIS CHAPTER knowing that the source material would come from the pages of my life. Behind me were years of ill-fated relationships, and here was a chance to share my experience in hopes that some of my fellow men might listen and avoid the mistakes I made. If what I have to say motivates even one prospective groom to think in greater depth than perhaps he already has on the long-range implications of his wedding, I will consider my efforts to have been a success.

Martha and I have been married for eleven years now and our life together is one of mutual admiration, respect, and a high degree of patience (certainly on Martha's part). Our little girls, Isabel (9) and Abigail (7), are the centerpieces of our life, our careers are ongoing, and for nine years we had the privilege of producing the television drama *Touched By An Angel,* which is still a ministry of hope for viewers around the world.

But things were not always so gratifying: Both Martha and I had lived with the anxiety of uncertain futures; each had experienced the vague sense of purposelessness that haunts the lives of so many people; and each had entered into relationships in haste and desperation only to emerge bruised but wiser. Aware of how easily a treasure can be squandered, we set about planning our

INVITING GOD TO YOUR WEDDING

new life together with the same attention to detail that we gave to the planning of our television show. Our livelihoods, and more importantly our reputations, depended on how skillfully we executed each episode. We would be no less as exacting in preparing ourselves for the event that would launch our future together.

We began the wedding planning with several suppositions: (1) that our culture has become far too casual about the institution of marriage; (2) that over time the rite has yielded more and more of its sacredness to showy ritual; (3) that the frequency of failed marriages is linked to the weakened values of our disposable society. Admittedly these are broad statements, but we felt that our challenges lay within them. Martha and I are far from perfect; there are things in our lives we wish we had done differently or not done at all, but we're stuck with our pasts—they are what they are, and there's nothing we can do to change them. What we can do, however, is influence the future.

This book is Martha's very personal vision. It consists, in part, of her reflections on the wedding that bound us together eleven years ago and is still remembered as a blessing to the lives of those who were there. When she shares her memories of that extraordinary day, her words resonate most vividly in the hearts of women. Men, on the other hand, appear less invested in the wedding ceremony itself—an observation that might be irrelevant if it didn't point to much bigger problems concerning the critical process of preparing for marriage. For the most part, men are left out of planning their weddings. But if a man is not profoundly involved in planning his marriage, its success in the long-term could be compromised, if not doomed.

For one thing, the benchmarks of character that once defined a husband have become so blurred that we're losing our cultural bearings. For example, where does a man go these days to gather the resources he needs to make a major life decision like marriage? Where will he sit in counsel with peers and elders and discuss the responsibilities of men in the context of family? Where and how does he prepare himself to be a good, reliable, effective husband and father? Sadly, he may not know that seeking guidance and support will make him stronger, not weaker.

Although sound preparation for marriage won't cure all our cultural ills, the provocative work of Pulitzer Prize–winning journalist Susan Faludi supports its importance to a society in the process of re-examining the roles of men. In her book *Stiffed,* she writes:

> The guiding standards of the fathers, the approving paternal eye, has nearly vanished in this barren new landscape, to be replaced by the market-share standards of a commercial culture, the ogling, ever restless eye of the camera. By the end of the century, every outlet of the consumer world—magazines, ads, movies, sports, music videos—would deliver the message that manhood had become a performance game to be won in the marketplace, not the workplace, and that male anger was now a part of the show; an ornamental culture that encouraged young men to see surliness, hostility and violence as expressions of glamour.

Faludi's work explores a complex set of problems that beset men in general, but it also implies that man's hope for the future may lie in redefining manhood. If, for example, we set ourselves against the trends she outlines and give serious consideration to what we can do as individuals to fortify our marriages, we have

a chance to control our own destinies instead of becoming vic-
tims of circumstance.

For many men—not only those planning to marry for the
first time, but those who have already struck out a time or
two—the whole idea of a wedding is a mystery. We believe it's
only women who have the emotional construct to handle it, so
we tend not to get involved. It is women who plan and execute
it, weeping tears of joy, while we look on, having laid all the
groundwork of a couple of cigars and a bachelor party. There's
an unmistakable gender gap in the process, the end result being
that men are less connected emotionally to their weddings than
women are. Unless he has a strong family, cultural, and/or religious framework where he can access tribal wisdom, the poor
fellow has only his own wits to count on, and that usually
involves his pride: "Don't worry, I've got this figured out . . . I
can handle it." The old saying "He who represents himself has a
fool for a lawyer" pertains fittingly to the man who, disdainful
of any authority higher than himself, decides he can figure out
marriage on his own. After all, love is eternally hopeful, and we
men tend to press on toward our wedding day sure that our special union can beat the odds and that romance and commitment
are all we need to hold it together. But hopeful imaginings are
no match for the often tumultuous interaction between two
people in love, and the noblest intentions can turn out to be
wishful thinking unless you, the man of the hour, create a level
playing field for the tests to come—and I assure you they will
come.

More basically, pride amounts to a kind of phantom
wisdom. Pride renders fools unteachable. They know

it all. You can't tell them anything. They are "wise in their own eyes"—a sure sign of folly. Badly educated ministers who are both vague and dogmatic, off-key singers who insist on contending for solo parts, children of Israel who wander forty years in the wilderness because even then the men were unwilling to ask for directions, pinball enthusiasts who devote ten years of their adult lives to becoming the best player in their neighborhood tavern, rejecting every inquiry into the worthwhileness of this project with the remark that the inquirer must be envious—these and other standouts from the ranks of the foolish display one of life's most wondrous combinations: the stubborn combination of ignorance and arrogance. The foolish, as the saying goes, are often in error but never in doubt. Moreover, when their dogmatism is challenged, they increase it. Some of them give you a piece of their mind they can hardly afford to lose.

CORNELIUS PLANTINGA, JR.
Not the Way It's Supposed to Be:
A Breviary of Sin

I included the above not to make sport of anyone's intelligence or characterize men as foolish, but to stress our vulnerability to overconfidence and lack of foresight. Pride has brought down many a promising marriage, and it's just one of the pitfalls we face. What I learned, I learned the hard way, and I feel a sense of duty to my fellow man to at least put up some guideposts where they can be seen.

DON'T GET MARRIED WITHOUT DOING YOUR HOMEWORK

Most of us give a respectful nod to the principle that the family unit is at the foundation of human life, but not everyone sees it as a living truth, let alone an imperative. All we have to do is pick up a newspaper or switch on the news to be reminded that something has gone terribly wrong. The divorce rate is a national catastrophe; we're so conditioned to the depressing statistics that we accept them without question, and our efforts to save the American family have accomplished little more than to maintain a status quo which, among its other depravities, is destroying whole segments of American youth. This cannot be what the Creator of the Universe intended. If one accepts that assumption, a question presents itself: What are we doing (or not doing) that sustains this seemingly inevitable cultural breakdown? I've come to the conclusion that my past marital problems began with my failure to address the meaning, purpose, and divine mystery of the wedding ceremony itself.

If we consider that one single hour will permanently alter the course of at least two lives, we would be well advised to do serious homework on the matter. God has provided us with clear direction, yet somewhere along the line we allowed the scriptural truths that guided our predecessors to slip away, and it's costing us dearly. It's more than mishap that so many of us wind up divorced, embittered, and broke. After all, we not only changed the rules, but we threw out the rule book. Religion and politics have become so intertwined in recent years that we'll likely spend the twenty-first century trying to sort out the mess; but we have to be careful not to throw the Bible out with the bathwater. The Bible contains a store of wisdom that has survived millennia of political history. Within its pages is the full range of human experience and emotion: war, peace, love, hate, betrayal, despair, devotion, hope, and encouragement. The Ten Commandments themselves provide a road map for successful living no matter what your religion; if we ignore them and lose our way, how do we get back?

> *If any of you lacks wisdom, he should ask God, who gives*
> *generously to all without finding fault, and it will be given*
> *to him. But when he asks, he must believe and not doubt,*
> *because he who doubts is like a wave of the sea, blown and*
> *tossed by the wind.*
>
> JAMES 1:5–6

I was never a quick study when it came to God; it took me decades to learn that unless I made His Word the central authority in my life, my chances of succeeding at anything of real importance would be slim indeed. In light of that discovery, it became clear that I had a lot of remedial work to do. Consider, for example, the way we approach marriage. Untrained and faced with a good chance of losing the most important relationship in our life, we bet our entire future on a single roll of the dice. (50 percent of first marriages, 67 percent of second, and 74 percent of third marriages end in divorce, according to Jennifer Baker of the Forest Institute of Professional Psychology in Springfield, Missouri.) That said, how does a man position himself to succeed at what is presumably the most momentous (and risky) undertaking of his life, given that he'll probably spend more time researching the car he's about to buy than planning for his marriage?

AVOID LOOKING FOR THE EMERGENCY
EXIT AS YOU APPROACH YOUR WEDDING

Most businessmen will agree that any issue vital to the success of an enterprise has to be considered with a blend of conservatism and boldness. In addition to caution and careful planning, a vision of how to achieve the desired outcome is not only essential, it's mandatory. From boyhood, males tend to think positively and aggressively when setting up projects—it's in our genes. So why, in this crucial area of our lives, do we consider failure an option?

In my own case, for example, the absence of mature guidance virtually guaranteed failure. My family was woefully deficient when it came to open communication, thus I had no idea what I was embarking upon when I decided to marry. I wasn't aware that I needed sound advice, and I might not have listened if it had been offered. More importantly, I was unprepared to deal with an insidious enemy that had long ago established its roots in me. By "enemy" I mean my own personal demons. Latent in most of us is the potential for at least some degree of self-destruction. It begins its life cycle as a thought that tempts us toward something questionable; then the thought becomes a whisper, and one day we may even act on its intention. If unopposed, it can direct our behavior, undermine our most important relationships, and ruin our lives. It feeds on negative conditioning we experienced in childhood, and from humble beginnings like fear, resentment, and jealousy, it may ripen into abuse, suicide, even murder. Its strongest ally is our natural inclination to deny its existence, and, like a virus, it confuses our efforts to counterattack by appearing in a variety of disguises. This enemy can not be underestimated, but if one is prepared and equipped, it can be neutralized.

> *Every good and excellent thing stands moment by moment*
> *on the edge of danger and must be fought for.*
> ATTRIBUTED TO THEODORE ROOSEVELT

In searching for my destiny in all the wrong places and always coming up short, I had become cynical and self-reliant. My success, I thought, was strictly a matter of my own intelligence and resourcefulness, and I enjoyed indulging that image. Façade, however, is of little use when one is on one's deathbed, which, at age fifty-five, is exactly where I found myself. After emergency abdominal surgery, stitched up like a Christmas goose with tubes coming out of everywhere, it was terrifyingly clear that nothing in the material world—not money, not friends, not family, not even my beloved resourcefulness—could get me out of this one. But it was a reading of the Twenty-third Psalm by an old Anglican priest who was visiting patients in the intensive care unit that gave me a glimpse of what real peace might be:

> *Yea, though I walk through the valley of the shadow of*
> *death, I will fear no evil; for thou art with me.*
> PSALM 23

Reverend Jim Veitch came every day, read from his old Bible, and eventually—and this is the best way I can describe the experience—my soul began to stir. In my broken state, alive only by God's grace and antibiotics, humility in its most elemental form was revealed to me. And this happened because I welcomed God into my life.

The intention of inviting God to your wedding is the subject of this book, and when the invitation has been extended, the next order of business is to enter into a relationship with Him.

PRAY HONESTLY AND SIMPLY, AS A CHILD TALKS TO A LOVING PARENT

By so doing, we enter into a process which, if sustained, becomes a central pillar of our marriage. It's the single point of communication where we're unlikely to engage in denial or self-deception. In that sanctified place, where we speak from our hearts instead of our heads, we discover the exhilarating freedom of complete openness with self and partner. In God's presence, we're free to examine ourselves as one would examine a bridge that needs maintenance: Where is it weak? Where is it structurally unsound? Where might the welds and rivets separate under pressure?

> *Isn't it strange*
> *That princes and kings,*
> *And clowns that caper*
> *In sawdust rings,*
> *And common people*
> *Like you and me*
> *Are builders for eternity?*
> *Each is given a bag of tools,*
> *A shapeless mass,*
> *A book of rules;*
> *And each must make—*
> *Ere life is flown—*
> *A stumbling block*
> *Or a steppingstone.*
>
> R. L. SHARPE

The intimacy you share with your beloved is as fragile as a spider's web. When love is threatened, ignored, manipulated, or betrayed, people become bitter, depressed, and angry. On any day of the week you'll find some media account of a tragedy that might have been avoided if God's counsel had been followed. A sound marriage is an exceptional and miraculous thing, but it's only as good as your determination to shepherd and protect it. This is where the rubber meets the road. This is where the shielding power of God's Word becomes your strength and your salvation as you prepare your spirit for the challenges to come. The quality of your life and the lives of your future generations rests squarely on your skill and determination as you prepare the ground for seeds you're about to sow.

PRAY WITH HER EVERY DAY

Take her hand; kneel before God; lift your voices in praise and gratitude for the gift of each other, and for the blessing of The Holy Spirit on your lives. My friend and brother in Christ, Tim Johnson, is a former defensive tackle for the Washington Redskins; he began his ministry counseling NFL football players and inner-city gang members in Washington, D.C., and now he pastors the Orlando World Outreach Center in Florida. I called on him when I started work on this chapter because his marriage to LeChelle is founded on unshakable faith in God's Word rather than their own views. He said this: "We must pray with humility—'Father, marriage is too big for me; the wisdom to make the right choices, to resolve conflicts, to deal with issues that could distract LeChelle and me from our devotion to one another is beyond me . . . I can't do it alone.' I grew up without a father and had to face that reality in my own marriage. I had no memory of a happy family in operation, no picture in my mind of a wholesome relationship between a man and a woman. How would I succeed without any points of reference?"

Tim, in revealing his own challenges, knew that the absence of a strong, loving male in his life was an issue that had to be dealt with, and he offers us this look at the path he followed: "If a man first applies himself to God and then to marriage, the will of God can find its way into his behavior. If I intend to become learned on the subject of marriage, I will enter into fellowship and counsel with married men of faith and ask them, how do I walk this out? How is it done? And when I'm invited to pray, I'll pray that God's will be done in my heart and in the heart of the woman I'm committing my life to. The transition from courtship to marriage means surrendering all I am and all I hope to be to LeChelle, as she likewise surrenders to me."

MEN: BEWARE THE SHADOWS OF YESTERDAY

Many of us have experienced family dysfunction and bear its scars. If our early memories are clouded with anger, pain, fear, and mistrust, what steps do we take to ensure that the past doesn't corrupt the future? It has been my experience that emotional life flows in channels carved out at a young age; something that triggered fear in me as a child may trigger it still. As an adult I've learned to mask it, but in certain situations it still elicits a response. For example, one of my mother's control devices was to turn her affection on and off like a faucet: "on," if I did what she wanted me to do, and "off" if I didn't. I have a clear memory of walking with her along a crowded sidewalk when I was about six years old and stopping to look in a store window; the delay apparently annoyed her and she walked off without me, presumably to teach me a lesson in keeping up. Although she quickly returned, lasting damage had been done. That ill-conceived lesson had destabilized my trust in the one person I

loved and needed most, and it was decades before my relationships with women stopped paying for the fear of abandonment
established before I could reason; its echo is still there.

The hearts and minds of children are new and vulnerable,
and a trauma, even an apparently minor one, can leave a lasting
mark. I strongly suggest, therefore, that anyone planning to
marry give wholehearted consideration to his or her own family
experience and ask the tough questions: When I was growing
up did an abuse cycle exist—either emotional or physical—that
might surface in my own marriage? Is there a negative tendency
in me that may have cropped up in previous relationships but
which I'm unwilling to address? Have I experienced a "family
secret," and if so will that secret and the lies accompanying it
shape my new life? The following scripture is among the sim-
plest and most profound expressions of wisdom available to a
parent, yet it's unknown in countless families.

> *And ye fathers, provoke not your children to wrath: but*
> *bring them up in the nurture and admonition of The Lord.*
>
> EPHESIANS 6:4

> *Fathers, do not embitter your children, or they will become*
> *discouraged.*
>
> COLOSSIANS 3:21

Our psyches are layered with pain inflicted in the past, and
emotionally healthy people learn to deal with it. However, the
ghosts of childhood often reappear when we start our own families. Under certain circumstances dark memories are not only
reawakened, but may find themselves in dreadfully familiar

territory; the ancient nightmare reanimates, perpetuating itself within the new family. Does this process fall into the category of things that define our dark side? Yes. Is it "the enemy" in manifestation? Yes.

> Marriage is a relationship in which a man and a woman protect and nurture the inner sanctum within and between them, and witness to that by the way in which they love each other. . . . The real mystery of marriage is not that husband and wife love each other so much that they can find God in each other's lives, but that God loves them so much that they can discover each other more and more as living reminders of His divine presence. They are brought together, indeed, as two prayerful hands extended toward God and forming in this way a home for Him in this world.
>
> HENRI NOUWEN
> *Clowning in Rome*

Good friends who cared about our future together and wanted to inspire us had that passage framed as a wedding gift. For the purposes of this discussion, however, we need to understand what it means in practice, to learn all we can about the weakness of our own flesh in order to gain control over it. There is no choice for thoughtful men but to develop a habit of spiritual alertness so we won't be knocked off our foundations every time our mate does something we don't like or says something we don't agree with—and these are the small things. We must learn how to handle not a bump, but a crater. We need to explore issues that are so tension-filled and so potentially explosive that they push buttons we forgot existed. I'm talking about emotions as treacherous as envy, as destructive as jealousy, as terrifying as suppressed rage, and the myriad evils they spawn. The enemy of marriage and family is formidable and well entrenched, but it can be brought under our control if we have the will and the courage to expose it to the light of God's truth.

IF YOU DON'T ADDRESS OLD HABITS OF ABUSE EARLY IN YOUR RELATIONSHIP, YOU WILL EVENTUALLY MISTREAT YOUR WIFE AND YOU WON'T BEHAVE ANY DIFFERENTLY TOWARD YOUR CHILDREN

During the year prior to our marriage, Martha and I committed ourselves to finding specific mechanisms that would help us maintain a balanced and happy married life. We knew from past failures that we had to root out anything in our own complicated natures that could endanger what we had; we weren't about to start our marriage without having explored, to the best of our ability, the problem areas. We spent hours working with a psychologist, and more hours in counsel with our trusted friend and pastor Jack Hayford. For nearly a year we prepared ourselves, bared our souls to one another, dismantled barriers to the working of God's will in our new life. By enriching our understanding of one another, we understood where we had to be when the excitement of the wedding had given way to the routine of everyday life.

COMMUNICATION

The strength of an emotional bond can be undermined by the unwillingness to communicate, and from the beginning we pledged to provide our own with maximum protection. Not everyone, however, feels comfortable opening up their innermost secrets for discussion, but the process is crucial for conflict resolution. Mutual respect hinges on telling the whole truth all the time, especially when dealing with deep and guarded matters. Steady communication is fundamental to any relationship, and most of us know the consequences of failing to maintain it. If our habit is to brood on our resentments, either reluctant or unable to reveal them to our future life partner, those resentments will incubate, and sooner or later something ugly will hatch. At this point we have handed the enemy the very weapon it needs to engineer our downfall. This adversary can then begin construction of a wall between you and your intended mate, and it will be you who provided footing, brick, and mortar. It takes time to complete such a wall, but if the lines of communication are down, you can be sure the work will go on.

> Be self-controlled and alert. Your enemy the devil prowls
> around like a roaring lion looking for someone to devour.
> Resist him, standing firm in the faith, because you know
> that your brothers throughout the world are undergoing the
> same kind of sufferings.
>
> 1 PETER 5:8–9

We've all known people who marry having not done the work required to establish communication as a habit. My friends and colleagues (we'll call them David and Beth) had, on the surface anyway, everything necessary for their upcoming marriage to succeed. They were educated, had promising careers, and both were gifted with charm and good looks. Nevertheless, both had ignored their own blind spots. In the heat and passion of their newfound love and hasty engagement, they responded to the encouraging voice that whispered, "What can possibly come between us?" They never considered that their future happiness would depend on more than brains and good looks, and they saw no reason to look for problems where none existed—certainly no reason to "go getting religious." Their wedding would be very cool, very hip, very unencumbered by pious sentiment. But there was darkness in David: a painful childhood recollection that he ignored to the point of denial, a recollection that eventually turned itself toward his intended mate. Even so, he would not and could not speak of it. During the period leading up to the wedding, David thought his fiancée was being overly attentive to his male friends. She was attractive, gregarious, possessed of a clever wit, and could usually be found at the center of a conversation. But the qualities that caught his fancy in the first place now began to irritate him—he was feeling twinges of jealousy and envy. The voice that whispered "nothing can possibly come between us," now awakened doubt and over time David found himself preoccupied with the notion that his fiancée was perhaps capable of betraying him. Since by now he couldn't conceive of life without her, his imaginings terrified him. He tried to ignore them, to silence them, to bury them, but the more he denied them the more powerful they became. Still he did not communicate his feelings to her—the wall was almost completed.

Some time after their wedding, Beth's boss gave a party. David, having downed a couple of martinis, thought he saw a spark of attraction between his wife and their host. The muddle of repressed anger that simmered in his brain eventually reached an alcohol-induced boil, and his mood turned dark. Finally he snapped, shoving his bride outside, where he began to berate her. Beth's boss, having seen the altercation, intervened on her behalf and sustained a punch in the mouth for his trouble. Beth lost her job; there followed a nasty divorce; and to make things worse, she was pregnant. Similar and more tragic scenarios are played out daily in our world. What could be more satisfying to an enemy engaged in the degradation of human life than to be regularly handed such golden opportunities?

> At the same time God binds things together, he binds humans to the rest of creation as stewards and care-takers of **it,** to himself as bearers of his image, and to each other as perfect complements—a matched pair of male and female persons who fit together and whose fitting harmony itself images God. Against a back-ground of original separating and binding, we must see the fall as anti-creation, the blurring of distinctions and the rupturing of bonds, and the one as a result of the other. Thus, human beings who want to be "like God, knowing good and evil" succeed only in alien-ating themselves from God and from each other. Even the good and fruitful earth becomes their foe (Gen. 3:17–18, cf. 4:12–14).
>
> CORNELIUS PLANTINGA, JR.
> *Not the Way It's Supposed to Be:*
> *A Breviary of Sin*

PATIENCE IS NOT ONLY AN EXPRESSION OF GOODNESS AND GENEROSITY, IT'S A REQUIREMENT FOR SURVIVAL

Having spent most of my life in the motion picture industry, where fear and loathing is the accepted modus operandi and patience is a rare commodity, I find that practicing it requires tremendous discipline. Countless industry brothers have fallen victim to stress-related ills such as high blood pressure, heart disease, stroke, tobacco addiction, and alcoholism, and I have long struggled with my own contentious nature. But until the certainty that I couldn't live without my wife struck me like a falling tree, nothing ever forced me to apply patience—except perhaps situations where my livelihood depended on keeping my mouth shut. Now, since we were about to take a vow before God promising to establish a genuinely new life for both of us, I had no choice but to retrain myself. The habit of displaying my vexation whenever I thought someone needed a blast of it had cost me in the past, and that habit would certainly not be well-received by Martha Williamson. So I decided to employ discretion (to the best of my ability) and thus avoid messy apologies—not to mention that I could no longer gamble my health on outbursts that might hasten my demise; I had a lot to live for. Impatience is insidious because it's so ordinary. For example, the workplace usually demands certain acceptance of a superior's temperament; his or her frustration over a subordinate's performance can be couched in edgy humor or disguised as a barbed correction, and there's not much to be done about it. But in a family it's not possible to conceal the intent of a snide remark or a brittle silence. The players know both the game and each other too well. In the lives of many people, impatience is synonymous with abuse, and it can lead to disaster. Consider someone you know—perhaps in your own family, perhaps even yourself—who does not acknowledge the pain he or she inflicts and who readily projects their frustrations upon those closest to them by applying criticism, spite, sarcasm, or ridicule. Then ask yourself some serious questions about your own behavior as it might apply to your future life partner.

1. Do my words or actions make her feel bad about herself? Or force her to be defensive?
2. Is there any area of our relationship where I cause discomfort or wherein she feels the need to be guarded in her opinions and responses?
3. Do I criticize or embarrass her in front of others?
4. Am I dismissive or evasive when she wants to discuss a problem?
5. Does she "take the blame" or work overtime to avoid my displeasure or anger?

If the answer to any of these questions is yes, your behavior may not be entirely in your control and you had better consider how you're going to deal with it. For the moment she may love you enough to put up with it, even overlook it, but will she continue to bear you as time goes on? A yes answer might be considered as a warning that your coming marriage might not make it over the long haul. Unless you are her sanctuary, the one place she feels wholly loved, protected, and most of all free, you cannot begin to secure your own future or to fulfill what God requires of you as a husband.

A gentle answer turns away wrath, but a harsh word stirs up anger.

PROVERBS 15:1

Out of the same mouth come praise and cursing. My brothers, this should not be. Can both fresh water and salt water flow from the same spring? My brothers, can a fig tree bear

*olives, or a grape vine bear figs? Neither can a salt spring
produce fresh water.*

JAMES 3:10–12

*A wife of noble character who can find? She is worth far
more than rubies.*

PROVERBS 31:10

I was never satisfied with the way I lived my life. I could
never shake the notion that something great might have happened if I had only handled things better. I had no idea, of
course, what I would have done differently; but what if I really
could start over? What if I could clean the slate and start life
anew? From time to time I sought God. I was an acolyte at Saint
Michael's and All Angels Episcopal Church in Southern
California when I was a boy; I studied the Sikh religion; I often
searched the Bible looking for inspiration; yet I never believed
in miracles. But that was then.

DON'T LEAVE PRAYER AS
THE LAST RESORT!

I never thought that the cliché *you have to hit bottom before you
can start back up* would apply to me, but after a year without
work, out of options and nearly broke, I was sinking into
depression. One night I wandered outside, stared up at the black
sky and whispered, "I haven't spoken to you for a long time,
Lord, but I want you to know that I'm a good television producer, and I'm available." An awkward prayer to be sure, and I
certainly wasn't counting on a response from the universe, but a
few days later I got a call from Bob Gros, an old friend and

production executive at CBS. To my surprise, he asked me to report for an interview with Martha Williamson, the executive producer of a new show called *Touched By An Angel*. "We'll shoot it in Salt Lake City," he said, "but don't let that bother you, it's about angels, I doubt if it'll last six episodes." That was in July of 1994. The show ran in the top ten for nine years, and in 1998 Martha and I were married.

SAN YSIDRO RANCH
SANTA BARBARA, CALIFORNIA

SATURDAY, FEBRUARY 14, 1998—5 A.M.

It was Valentine's Day. I awoke to the sound of rain lashing the windows of my cabin, and a sharp crack of thunder sat me bolt upright. "The tent," I thought, as I fumbled in the dark for the light switch and hurried to get into my clothes. California was experiencing the heaviest winter storms in decades, and the coast was taking the worst of it. Roads were disappearing, houses were sliding into the sea, and the earth from Point Conception to the Mexican border was completely saturated. It was my wedding day. Twelve hours from now, if the big tent we set up as a church was still standing and if Pastor Hayford's car could get through on Pacific Coast Highway, Martha and I would be wed.

Drenched, I stumbled around the perimeter of the wedding tent, tugging at the huge steel tent pegs I had insisted on using. The ground had turned to mud, but the extra long pegs had been driven in deep and were holding, at least for the moment. Inside the tent, however, things had taken a turn for the worse. A gutter designed to carry rainwater away from the tent had failed, and the carpeted floor of our little church was awash in two inches of water. The vulnerable construction was leaking and creaking; tent ropes were stretched to their limits, and I imagined scenarios of the whole thing crashing down on top of the ceremony. It had occurred to me two weeks ago when our wedding coordinator panicked and quit, having accomplished next to nothing, that we'd asked too much of her. In hindsight, I should have abandoned the idea of erecting and decorating our own wedding chapel, reception hall, and cigar and cognac bar when I had the chance, but by then it was too late to turn back. So, I called my friend Fred Weiler, a well respected studio production designer from Daytona Beach. "Buddy, I've got a challenge here. I need a church . . . it has to be dressed and ready in two weeks." He asked me the name of the show and I answered, "It's not exactly a show, it's my wedding." So, Fred left Daytona Beach for the coast, set up shop at San Ysidro Ranch, and was soon nicknamed "Fredrick of Florida," Santa Barbara's newest mega-wedding specialist.

8 A.M.

Workers have repaired the failed rain gutter and are vacuuming up the last of the water from the church floor. There's a momentary lull in the storm, the roads are still open, the flowers have arrived, and my blood pressure is starting to go down. "I think I'll get away for a while, turn it over to God, stop thinking about all the things that could still go wrong and just give thanks for the miracle that's unfolding." I picture Martha gliding down the aisle in her wedding dress, which calms me down.

> *Give thanks to the Lord, call on His name; make known*
> *among the nations what He has done.*
>
> PSALMS 105:1

11 A.M.

I try to shut out the sound of the rain, to accept the fact that it's actually happening and not my imagination. But it's true. I'm about to be married in the presence of Almighty God to the woman I love. The day has a supernatural gravity to it, like what you feel at a birth or a death. That's it! The old, fearful man is about to die and a new man is about to be born. The Lord has blessed me with the chance to do it right.

> *My son, keep my words, and treasure my commands within you. Keep my commands and live, and my law as the apple of your eye. Bind them on your fingers; write them on the tablet of your heart.*
>
> PROVERBS 7:1–3

4 P.M.

It has taken a full hour to get dressed, and half of that time was consumed fumbling with my bow tie. But I'm keeping focused by thinking simple thoughts and doing simple things like pacing up and down. Bob Gros, my groomsman, is at the door, his face ashen. "I forgot my cuff links and studs." I tell him to use paper clips. He stands there stunned, but the blood returns to his face when I produce a spare set I stashed just in case. He leaves, and I notice that there are barely discernable breaks in the clouds; the rain is subsiding. "Lord, hold back the next downpour."

5 P.M.

The moment has arrived and the wedding begins. Wind is whistling through the ropes and whipping at the tent where 150

friends and family members are gathered. A perfect double rainbow has formed over the wedding tent. Crows in a tree outside
have set up a cacophonous chorus of their own, and suddenly
I'm at the altar waiting for Martha. Every dream we had, every
prayer we uttered, everything we did together to bring honor,
substance, and power to this moment is about to be sealed upon
us in the presence of God. The music surges, the doors open
wide and she appears; smiling, joyful, radiant.

> *You have stolen my heart, my sister, my bride;*
> *you have stolen my heart*
> *with one glance of your eyes,*
> *with one jewel of your necklace.*
> *How delightful is your love, my sister,*
> *my bride.*
> *How much more pleasing is your love*
>   *than wine,*
> *And the fragrance of your perfume than any spice!*
> *Your lips, oh my bride,*
> *drip sweetness as the honeycomb;*
> *milk and honey are under your tongue;*
> *you are a garden fountain,*
> *a well of living waters*
> *streaming down from Lebanon.*
>   SONG OF SONGS 4:9–11, 15

Wake up in the morning with a blessing for each
other—even if it's just a word of gratitude for being
able to be together one more morning. Return home
with a blessing for each other—some beauty, grace, or

kindness that you experienced in the day. Protect yourself from the theft of that special light by setting aside
time for sacred events: for the Shabbat, the Sabbath
day, for other holy days, for doing things apart from
your professional work that keep you aware that you
are not defined solely by the work you do. And
remember that everywhere you go, your life together
will be seen as a blessing if you so will it. That was the
task assigned Abraham and Sarah in the beginning of
our people: "Be thou a blessing," God says in the
Book of Genesis.

RABBI LARRY PINSKER
Toronto, Ontario

In closing, may I ask three things of you? First, that you think
on God's promise: *"For I know the thoughts that I think toward you,
thoughts of peace and not of evil, to give you a future and a hope."* And
second, that you pray for the courage to include God in your
wedding plans and in your marriage. And finally, I ask that as
you begin your married life you seal in your hearts His words:
"Be thou a blessing."

Martha and I extend our love, and may God be with you
always.

JON ANDERSEN

Permissions

About the Author

As Executive Producer of CBS's *Touched By An Angel*, Martha Williamson became widely recognized as a television pioneer when her series about the love of God grew a weekly audience of more than 24 million viewers and remained a staple on the network for nine years. Following her successful spin-off, *Promised Land,* she became the first woman to solely produce two network television dramas simultaneously. *Touched By An Angel* was nominated for nine Emmy Awards and was inducted into the Museum of Television and Radio Hall of Fame. It has been translated into more than sixty languages and continues to be broadcast around the world. Named in 2007 by Beliefnet.com as one of the Ten Most Powerful Christians in Hollywood, Martha has been honored with the Freedom Works Award from the United States Congress, the Edward R. Murrow Responsibility in Television Award, the Producers Guild Nova Award, the Templeton Prize, as well as honors from the Anti-Defamation League, the NAACP, Catholics in Media, and others. She was appointed to the President's White House Council on Service and Civic Participation and serves on the Board of Directors for the Pasadena Playhouse. Her numerous television appearances include *60 Minutes, Larry King Live,* and *Oprah.*

A popular speaker, she has appeared onstage on both coasts performing her musical one-woman show *Martha at Risk* with Tony Award–winning composer Larry Grossman. Martha Williamson is the host and voice of "A Touch of Encouragement," on

Beliefnet.com. She lives in Southern California with her husband, Jon Andersen, and their two daughters. Martha is a graduate of Williams College and is a recipient of the Williams Bicentennial Medal.